THE EFFECTIVE EXECUTIVE

Other books by Peter F. Drucker

Management

Post-capitalist Society
Managing for the Future
Managing the Non-profit Organization
The Frontiers of Management
Innovation and Entrepreneurship
Management: Tasks, Responsibilities, Practices
The Practice of Management
Managing for Results
The Changing World of the Executive
Managing in Turbulent Times
The New Markets and Other Essays
Concept of the Corporation

Economics, politics, society

The Ecological Vision
The New Realities
Toward the Next Economics
The Unseen Revolution
Men, Ideas and Politics
The Age of Discontinuity
The Landmarks of Tomorrow
America's Next Twenty Years
The New Society
The Future of Industrial Man
The End of Economic Man

Fiction

The Temptation to Do Good
The Last of All Possible Worlds

Autobiography

Adventures of a Bystander

The Effective Executive

PETER F. DRUCKER

Butterworth-Heinemann

An Imprint of Elsevier

THE EFFECTIVE EXECUTIVE
Peter F. Drucker

Butterworth-Heinemann
An Imprint of Elsevier
Linacre House, Jordan Hill, Oxford OX2 8DP
225 Wildwood Avenue, Woburn, MA 01801-2041

Classic Edition 2000

International Standard Book Number: 0-7506-4869-4

First Printed in India 2004

Indian Reprint ISBN: 81-8147-378-7

Published by Elsevier, a division of Reed Elsevier India Pvt. Ltd., 17-A/1, Main Ring Road, Lajpat Nagar IV, New Delhi - 110 024.

Printed and bound in India by
Rajkamal Electric Press, B-35/9 G.T.Karnal Road Delhi-110033

Contents

Preface

Management books usually deal with managing other people. The subject of this book is managing oneself for effectiveness. That one can truly manage other people is by no means adequately proven. But one can always manage oneself. Indeed, executives who do not manage themselves for effectiveness cannot possibly expect to manage their associates and subordinates. Management is largely by example. Executives who do not know how to make themselves effective in their own job and work set the wrong example.

To be reasonably effective it is not enough for the individual to be intelligent, to work hard or to be knowledgeable. Effectiveness is something separate, something different. But to be effective also does not require special gifts, special aptitude, or special training. Effectiveness as an executive demands *doing* certain – and fairly simple – things. It consists of a small number of practices, the practices that are presented and discussed in this book. But these practices are not 'inborn'. In forty-five years of work as a consultant with a large number of executives in a wide variety of organizations – large and small; businesses, government agencies, labor unions, hospitals, universities, community services; American, European, Latin American and Japanese – I have not come across a single 'natural': an executive who was born effective. All the effective ones have had to learn to be effective. And all of them then had to practice effectiveness until it became habit. But all the ones who worked on making themselves effective executives succeeded in doing so. Effectiveness can be learned – and it also *has* to be learned.

Effectiveness is what executives are being paid for, whether they work as managers who are responsible for the performance of others as well as their own, or as individual professional contributors responsible for their own performance only. Without effectiveness there is no 'performance', no matter how much intelligence and knowledge goes into the work, no matter how many hours it takes. Yet it is perhaps not too surprising that we have so far paid little attention to the effective executive. Organizations – whether business enterprises, large government agencies, labor unions, large hospitals or large universities – are, after all, brand new. A century ago almost no one had even much contact with such organizations beyond an occasional trip to the local post office to mail a letter. And effectiveness as an executive means effectiveness in and through an organization. Until recently there was little reason for anyone to pay much attention to the effective executive or to worry about the low effectiveness of so many of them. Now, however, most people – especially those with even a fair amount of schooling – can expect to spend all their working lives in an organization of some kind. Society has become a society of organizations in all developed countries. Now the effectiveness of the individual depends increasingly on his or her ability to be effective in an organization, to be effective as an executive. And the effectiveness of a modern society and its ability to perform – perhaps even its ability to survive – depend increasingly on the effectiveness of the people who work as executives in the organizations. The effective executive is fast becoming a key resource for society, and effectiveness as an executive a prime requirement for individual accomplishment and achievement – for young people at the beginning of their working lives fully as much as for people in mid-career.

Claremont, California
New Year's Day, 1987

Peter F. Drucker

1

Effectiveness Can be Learned

To be effective is the job of the executive. 'To effect' and 'to execute' are, after all, near-synonyms. Whether he works in a business or in a hospital, in a government agency or in a labour union, in a university or in the army, the executive is, first of all, expected to *get the right things done*. And this is simply saying that he is expected to be effective.

Yet men of high effectiveness are conspicuous by their absence in executive jobs. High intelligence is common enough among executives. Imagination is far from rare. The level of knowledge tends to be high. But there seems to be little correlation between a man's effectiveness and his intelligence, his imagination or his knowledge. Brilliant men are often strikingly ineffectual; they fail to realize that the brilliant insight is not by itself achievement. They never have learned that insights become effectiveness only through hard systematic work. Conversely, in every organization there are some highly effective plodders. While others rush around in the frenzy and busyness which very bright people so often confuse with 'creativity', the plodder puts one foot in front of the other and gets there first, like the tortoise in the old fable.

Intelligence, imagination, and knowledge are essential resources, but only effectiveness converts them into results. By themselves, they only set limits to what can be attained.

I. Why we Need Effective Executives

All this should be obvious. But why then has so little attention been paid to effectiveness in an age in which there are mountains of books and articles on every other aspect of the executive's tasks?

One reason for this neglect is that effectiveness is the specific technology of the knowledge worker within an organization. Until very recently, there was no more than a handful of these around.

For manual work, we need only efficiency; that is, the ability to do things right rather than the ability to get the right things done. The manual worker can always be judged in terms of the quantity and quality of a definable and discrete output, such as a pair of shoes. How to measure efficiency and how to define quality in manual work we have learned during the last hundred years – to the point where we have been able tremendously to multiply the output of the individual worker.

Formerly, the manual worker – whether machine operator or front-line soldier – predominated in all organizations. Few people of effectiveness were needed: those at the top who gave the orders that others carried out. They were so small a fraction of the total work population that we could, rightly or wrongly, take their effectiveness for granted. We could depend on the supply of 'naturals', the few people in any area of human endeavour who somehow know what the rest of us have to learn the hard way.

This was true not only of business and the Army. It is hard to realize today that 'government' during the American Civil War a hundred years ago meant the merest handful of people. Lincoln's Secretary of War had fewer than fifty civilian subordinates, most of them not 'executives' and policy-makers but telegraph clerks. The entire Washington establishment of the U.S. government in Theodore Roosevelt's time, that is around 1900, could be comfortably housed in any one of the government buildings along the Mall today.

The hospital of yesterday did not know any of the 'health-service professionals', the X-ray and lab technicians, the dieticians and therapists, the social workers, and so on, of whom it now employs as many as 250 for every 100 patients. Apart from a few nurses, there were only cleaning women, cooks, and maids. The physician was the knowledge worker, with the nurse as his aide.

In other words, up to recent times, the major problem of organization was efficiency in the performance of the manual worker who did what he had been told to do. Knowledge workers were not predominant in organization.

In fact, only a small fraction of the knowledge workers of earlier days were part of an organization. Most of them worked by themselves as professionals, at best with a clerk. Their effectiveness or lack of effectiveness concerned only themselves and affected only themselves.

Today, however, the large knowledge organization is the central reality. Modern society is a society of large organized institutions. In every one of them, including the armed services, the centre of gravity has shifted to the knowledge worker, the man who puts to work what he has between his ears rather than the brawn of his muscles or the skill of his hands. Increasingly, the majority of people who have been schooled to use knowledge, theory, and concept rather than physical force or manual skill work in an organization and are effective only in so far as they can make a contribution to the organization.

Now effectiveness can no longer be taken for granted. Now it can no longer be neglected.

The imposing system of measurements and tests which we have developed for manual work – from industrial engineering to quality control – is not applicable to knowledge work. There are few things less pleasing to the Lord, and less productive, than an engineering department that rapidly turns out beautiful blueprints for the wrong product. Working on the *right* things is what makes knowledge work effective. This is not capable of being measured by any of the yardsticks for manual work.

The knowledge worker cannot be supervised closely or in detail. He can only be helped. But he must direct himself, and he must direct himself toward performance and contribution, that is toward effectiveness.

> A cartoon in *The New Yorker* magazine some time ago showed an office on the door of which was the legend: 'Chas. Smith, General Sales Manager, Ajax Soap Company.' The walls were bare except for a big sign saying 'Think'. The man in the office had his feet propped up on his desk and was blowing smoke rings at the ceiling. Outside two older men went by, the one saying to the other: 'But how can we be sure that Smith thinks soap?'

One can indeed never be sure what the knowledge worker thinks – and yet thinking is his specific work, it is his 'doing'.

The motivation of the knowledge worker depends on his being effective, on his being able to achieve.* If effectiveness is lacking

* This is brought out in all studies, especially in three empirical works: Frederick Herzberg (with B. Mauser and B. Snyderman), *The Motivation To Work* (New York, Wiley, 1959); David C. McClellan, *The Achieving Society* (Princeton, N.J. Van Nostrand, 1961); and Frederick Herzberg, *Work And The Nature Of Man* (Cleveland, World, 1966).

in his work, his commitment to work and to contribution will soon wither, and he will become a time-server going through the motions from 9 to 5.

The knowledge worker does not produce something that is effective by itself. He does not produce a physical product – a ditch, a pair of shoes, a machine part. He produces knowledge, ideas, information. By themselves these 'products' are useless. Somebody else, another man of knowledge, has to take them as his input and convert them into his output before they have any reality. The greatest wisdom not applied to action and behaviour is meaningless data. The knowledge worker, therefore, must do something which a manual worker need not do. He must provide effectiveness. He cannot depend on the utility his output carries with it as does a well-made pair of shoes.

The knowledge worker is the one 'factor of production' through which the highly developed societies and economies of today – the United States, Western Europe, Japan, and also increasingly, the Soviet Union – become and remain competitive.

This is particularly true of the United States. The only resource in respect to which America can possibly have a competitive advantage is education. American education may leave a good deal to be desired. But it is massive beyond anything poorer societies can afford. For education is the most expensive capital investment we have ever known. A Ph.D. in the natural sciences represents $100,000 to $200,000 of social capital investment. Even the boy who graduates from college without any specific professional competence represents an investment of $50,000 or more. This only a very rich society can afford.

Education is the one area, therefore, in which the richest of all societies, the United States, has a genuine advantage – provided it can make the knowledge worker productive. And productivity for the knowledge worker means the ability to get the right things done. It means effectiveness.

II. Who Is an Executive?

Every knowledge worker in modern organization is an executive if, by virtue of his position or knowledge, he is responsible for a contribution that materially affects the capacity of the organization to perform and to obtain results. This may be the capacity of a business to bring out a new product or to obtain a larger share of a given market. It may be the capacity of a hospital to provide bedside care to its patients, and so on. Such a man (or woman) must make decisions; he cannot just carry out orders. He must take responsiblity for his contribution. And he is supposed, by virtue of his knowledge, to be better equipped to make the right decision than anyone else. He may be over-ridden; he may be demoted or fired. But so long as he has the job, so long the goals, the standards, and the contribution are in his keeping.

Most managers are executives – though not all. But many non-managers are also becoming executives in modern society. For the knowledge organization, as we have been learning these last few years, needs *both* 'managers' and 'individual professional contributors' in positions of responsibility, decision-making, and authority.

This fact is perhaps best illustrated by a recent newspaper interview with a young American infantry captain in the Vietnam jungle.

> Asked by the reporter, 'how in this confused situation can you retain command?', the young captain said: 'Around here, I am only the guy who is responsible. If these men don't know what to do when they run into an enemy in the jungle, I'm too far away to tell them. My job is to make sure they know. What they do depends on the situation which only they can judge. The responsibility is always mine, but the decision lies with whoever is on the spot.'

In a guerrilla war, every man is an 'executive'.

There are many managers who are not executives. Many people, in other words, are superiors of other people – and often of fairly large numbers of other people – and still do not seriously affect the ability of the organization to perform. Most foremen in a manufacturing plant belong here. They are 'overseers' in the literal sense of the word. They are 'managers' in that they manage the work of others. But they have neither the responsibility for, nor authority over, the direction, the content, and the quality of the work, or the methods of its performance. They can still be measured and appraised very largely in terms of efficiency and quality, and by the yardsticks we have developed to measure and appraise the work and performance of the manual worker.

Conversely, whether a knowledge worker is an executive does not depend on whether he manages people or not. In one business, the market research man may have a staff of 200 people, whereas the market research man of the closest competitor is all by himself and has only a secretary for his staff. This should make little difference in the contribution expected of the two men. It is an administrative detail. Two hundred people, of course, can do a great deal more work than one man. But it does not follow that they produce and contribute more.

Knowledge work is not defined by quantity. Neither is knowledge work defined by its costs. Knowledge work is defined by its results. And for these, the size of the group and the magnitude of the managerial job are not even symptoms.

Having many people working in market research may endow the results with that increment of insight, imagination, and quality that gives a company the potential of rapid growth and success. If so, 200 men are cheap. But it is just as likely that the manager will be overwhelmed by all the problems 200 men bring to their work and cause through their interactions. He may be so busy 'managing' as to have no time for market research and for fundamental decisions. He may be so busy checking figures that he never asks the question: 'What do we really mean when we say "our market"?' And as a result, he may fail to notice significant changes in the market which eventually may cause the downfall of his company.

But the individual market researcher without a staff may be equally productive or unproductive. He may be the source of the knowledge and vision that make his company prosper. Or he may spend so much of his time hunting down details – the footnotes academicians so often mistake for 'research' – as to see and hear nothing and to think even less. Throughout every one of our knowledge organizations, we have people who manage no one and yet are executives. Rarely indeed do we find a situation such as that in the Vietnam jungle, where at any moment, any member of the entire group may be called upon to make decisions with life-and-death impact for the whole. But the chemist in the research laboratory who decides to follow one line of inquiry rather than another one may make the entrepreneurial decision that determines the future of his company. He may be the research director. But he also may be – and often is – a chemist with no managerial responsibilities, if not even a fairly junior man. Similarly, the decision what to consider one 'product' in the account books* may be made by a senior vice-president in the company. It may also be made by a junior. And this holds true in all areas of today's large organization.

I have called 'executives' those knowledge workers, managers, or individual professionals, who are expected, by virtue of their position or their knowledge, to make decisions in the normal course of their work that have significant impact on the performance and results of the whole. They are by no means a majority of the knowledge workers. For in knowledge work too, as in all others areas, there is unskilled work and routine. But they are a much larger proportion of the total knowledge-work force than any organization chart ever reveals.

This is beginning to be realized† – as witness the many attempts to provide parallel ladders of recognition and reward for managers and for individual professional contributors. What few yet realize, however, is how many people there are even in the most humdrum organization of today, whether business or government agency, research lab or hospital, who have to make decisions of significant and irreversible impact. For the authority of knowledge is surely as legitimate as the authority of position.

These decisions, moreover, are of the same *kind* as the decisions of top management. (This was the main point Mr Kappel was making in the statement referred to above.)

The most subordinate manager, we now know, may do the same kind of work as the president of the company or the administrator of the government agency: that is, plan, organize, integrate, motivate, and measure. His compass may be quite limited. But within his sphere, he is an executive.

Similarly, every decision-maker does the same kind of work as the company president or the administrator. His scope may be quite limited. But he is an executive even if his function or his name appear neither on the organization chart nor in the internal telephone directory.

* On this see my *Managing For Results* (New York, Harper and Row; London, Heinemann, 1964) – especially Chapter 2.

† The best statement I know was made by Frederick R. Kappel, the head of the American Telephone & Telegraph Company (The Bell Telephone System) at the XIIIth International Management Congress in New York, September 1963. Mr Kappel's main points are quoted in Chapter 14 of my book *Managing For Results*.

And whether chief executive or beginner, he needs to be effective.

Many of the examples used in this book are taken from the work and experience of chief executives – in government, army, hospitals, business, and so on. The main reason is that these are accessible, are indeed often on the public record. Also big things are more easily analysed and seen than small ones.

But the book itself is not a book on what people at the top do or should do. It is addressed to every one who, as a knowledge worker, is responsible for actions and decisions which are meant to contribute to the performance capacity of his organization. It is meant for every one of the men I call 'executives'.

III. Executive Realities

The realities of the executive's situation both demand effectiveness from him and make effectiveness exceedingly difficult to achieve. Indeed, unless executives work at becoming effective, the realities of their situation will push them into futility.

Take a quick look at the realities of a knowledge worker *outside* an organization to see the problem. A physician has by and large no problem of effectiveness. The patient who walks into his office brings with him everything to make the physician's knowledge effective. During the time he is with the patient, the doctor can, as a rule, devote himself to the patient. He can keep interruptions to a minimum. The contribution the physician is expected to make is clear. What is important, and what is not, is determined by whatever ails the patient. The patient's complaints establish the doctor's priorities. And the goal, the objective, is given. It is to restore the patient to health or at least to make him more comfortable. Physicians are not noted for their capacity to organize themselves and their work. But few of them have much trouble being effective.

The executive in organization is in an entirely different position. In his situation there are four major realities over which he has essentially no control. Every one of them is built into organization and into the executive's day and work. He has no choice but to 'co-operate with the inevitable'. But every one of these realities exerts pressure toward non-results and non-performance.

1. The executive's time tends to belong to everybody else. If

one attempted to define an 'executive' operationally (that is, through his activities) one would have to define him as a captive of the organization. Everybody can move in on his time, and everybody does. There seems to be very little any one executive can do about it. He cannot, as a rule, stick his head out of the door and say to the nurse: 'I won't see anybody for the next half hour.' Just at this moment, his phone rings, and he has to speak to the company's best customer or to a high official in the city administration or to his boss – and the next half hour is already gone.

This comes out clearly in the one study of top management in large corporations which actually recorded the time use of senior executives.* Even the most effective executives in Professor Carlson's study found most of their time taken up with the demands of others and for purposes which added little if anything to their effectiveness. In fact, executives might well be defined as people who normally have no time of their own, because their time is always pre-empted by matters of importance to somebody else.

2. Executives are forced to keep on 'operating' unless they take positive action to change the reality in which they live and work.

In the United States, the complaint is common that the company president – or any other senior officer – still continues to run marketing or the plant, even though he is now in charge of the whole business and should be giving his time to its direction. This is sometimes blamed on the fact that American executives graduate, as a rule, out of functional work and operations, and cannot slough off the habits of a lifetime when they get into general management. But exactly the same complaint can be heard in countries where the career ladder is quite different. In the Germanic countries, for instance, a common route into top management has been from a central secretariat, where one works all along as a 'generalist'. Yet in German, Swedish, or Dutch companies top management people are criticized just as much for operating as in the U.S. Nor, when one looks at organizations, is this tendency confined to the top; it pervades the entire executive group. There must be a reason for this tendency to 'operate' other than career ladders or even the general perversity of human nature.

* Sune Carlson, *Executive Behavior* (Strombergs, Stockholm, 1951).

The fundamental problem is the reality around the executive. Unless he changes it by deliberate action, the flow of events will determine what he is concerned with and what he does.

Depending on the flow of events is appropriate for the physician. The doctor who looks up when a patient comes in and says: 'Why are you here today?' expects the patient to tell him what is relevant. When the patient says, 'Doctor, I can't sleep. I haven't been able to go to sleep the last three weeks,' he is telling the doctor what the priority area is. Even if the doctor decides, upon closer examination, that the sleeplessness is a fairly minor symptom of a much more fundamental condition he will do something to help the patient to get a few good nights' rest.

But events rarely tell the executive anything, let alone the real problem. For the doctor, the patient's complaint is central because it is central to the patient. The executive is concerned with a much more complex universe. What events are important and relevant and what events are merely distractions, the events themselves do not indicate. They are not even symptoms in the sense in which the patient's narrative is a clue for the physician.

If the executive lets the flow of events determine what he does, what he works on and what he takes seriously, he will fritter himself away operating. He may be an excellent man. But he is certain to waste his knowledge and ability and to throw away what little effectiveness he might have achieved. What the executive needs are criteria which enable him to work on the truly important, that is on contributions and results, even though the criteria are not found in the flow of events.

3. The third reality pushing the executive toward ineffectiveness is that he is within an *organization*. This means that he is effective only if and when other people make use of what he contributes. Organization is a means of multiplying the strength of an individual. It takes his knowledge and uses it as the resource, the motivation, and the vision of other knowledge workers. Knowledge workers are, however, rarely in phase with each other, precisely because they are knowledge workers. Each has his own skill and his own concerns. One man may be interested in taxes, or in bacteriology, or in training and developing tomorrow's key administrators in the city government. But the fellow next door is interested in the finer points of cost accounting, in hospital economics, or in the legalities of the city charter. Each has to be able to use what the other produces.

Usually, the people who are most important to the effectiveness of an executive are not people over whom he has direct control. They are people in other areas, people who in terms of organization, are 'sideways'. Or they are his superiors. Unless the executive can reach these people, can make his contribution effective for them and in their work, he has no effectiveness at all.

4. Finally, the executive is *within* an organization.

Every executive, whether his organization is a business or a research laboratory, a government agency, a large university, or the air force, sees the inside, the organization, as close and immediate reality. He sees the outside only through thick and distorting lenses, if at all. What goes on outside is usually not even known first-hand. It is received through an organizational filter of reports, that is in an already pre-digested and highly abstract form that imposes organizational criteria of relevance on the outside reality.

But the organization is an abstraction. Mathematically, it would have to be represented as a point – that is as having neither size nor extension. Even the largest organization is unreal compared to the reality of the environment in which it exists.

Specifically, there are no results within the organization. All the results are on the outside. The only business results, for instance, are produced by a customer who converts the costs and efforts of the business into revenues and profits through his willingness to exchange his purchasing power for the products or services of the business. The customer may make his decisions as a consumer on the basis of market considerations of supply and demand, or as a socialist government which regulates supply and demand on the basis of essentially non-economic value preferences. In either case the decision-maker is outside rather than inside the business.

Similarly, a hospital has results only in respect to the patient. But the patient is not a member of the hospital organization. For the patient, the hospital is 'real' only while he stays there. His greatest desire is to go back to a hospital-free world as fast as possible.

What happens inside any organization is effort and cost. To

speak of 'profit centres' in a business as we are wont to do is polite euphemism. There are only effort centres. The less an organization has to do to produce results, the better it does its job. That it takes 100,000 employees to produce the automobiles or the steel the market wants is essentially a gross engineering imperfection. The fewer people, the smaller, the less activity inside, the more nearly perfect is the organization in terms of its only reason for existence: the service to the environment.

This outside, this environment which is the true reality, is well beyond effective control from the inside. At the most, results are co-determined, as for instance in warfare, where the outcome is the result of the actions and decisions of both armies. In a business, there can be attempts to mould the customers' preferences and values through promotion and advertising. Except in an extreme shortage situation such as a war economy, the customer still has the final word and the effective veto power (which explains why every communist economy has run into trouble as soon as it moved beyond extreme shortages and long before it reached a position of adequate market supply in which the customer, rather than the political authorities, makes the real and final decisions).

But it is the inside of the organization that is most visible to the executive. It is the inside that has immediacy for him. Its relations and contacts, its problems and challenges, its cross-currents and gossip reach him and touch him at every point. Unless he makes special efforts to gain direct access to outside reality, he will become increasingly inside-focused. The higher up in the organization he goes, the more will his attention be drawn to problems and challenges of the inside rather than to events on the outside.

An organization, a social artifact, is very different from a biological organism. Yet it stands under the law that governs the structure and size of animals and plants: the surface goes up with the square of the radius, but the mass grows with the cube. The larger the animal becomes, the more resources have to be devoted to the mass and to the internal tasks, to circulation and information, to the nervous system, and so on.

Every part of an amoeba is in constant, direct contact with the environment. It therefore needs no special organs to perceive its environment or to hold it together. But a large and complex animal such as man needs a skeleton to hold it together. It needs all kinds of specialized organs for ingestion and digestion, for respiration and exhalation, for carrying oxygen to the tissues, for reproduction, and so on. Above all, a man needs a brain and a number of complex nervous systems. Most of the mass of the amoeba is directly concerned with survival and procreation. Most of the mass of the higher animal, its resources, its food, its energy supply, its tissues, serve to overcome and offset the complexity of the structure and the isolation from the outside.

An organization is not, like an animal, an end in itself, and successful by the mere act of perpetuating the species. An organization is an organ of society and fulfils itself by the contribution it makes to the outside environment. And yet the bigger and apparently more successful an organization gets to be, the more will inside events tend to engage the interests, the energies, and the abilities of the executive to the exclusion of his real tasks and his real effectiveness in the outside.

This danger is being aggravated today by the advent of the computer and of the new information technology. The computer, being a mechanical moron, can handle only quantifiable data. These it can handle with speed, accuracy, and precision. It will, therefore, grind out hitherto unobtainable quantified information in large volume. One can, however, by and large quantify only what goes on inside an organization – costs and production figures, patient statistics in the hospital, or training reports. The relevant outside events are rarely available in quantifiable form until it is much too late to do anything about them.

This is not because our information-gathering capacity in respect to the outside events lags behind the technical abilities of the computer. If this were the only thing to worry about, we would just have to increase statistical efforts – and the computer itself would greatly help us to overcome this mechanical limitation. The problem is rather that the important and relevant outside events are often qualitative and not capable of quantification. They are not yet 'facts'. For a fact, after all, is an event which somebody has defined, has classified and, above all, has endowed with relevance. To be able to quantify one has to have a concept first. One first has to abstract from the infinite welter of phenomena a specific aspect which one then can name and finally count.

The Thalidomide tragedy which led to the birth of so many

deformed babies is a case in point. By the time doctors on the European continent had enough statistics to realize that the number of deformed babies born was significantly larger than normal – so much larger that there had to be a specific and new cause – the damage had been done. In the United States, the damage was prevented because one public-health physician perceived a qualitative change – a minor and by itself meaningless skin tingling caused by the drug – related it to a totally different event that had happened many years earlier, and sounded the alarm before Thalidomide actually came into use.

The Ford Edsel holds a similar lesson. All the quantitative figures that could possibly be obtained were gathered before the Edsel was launched. All of them pointed to its being the right car for the right market. The qualitative change – the shifting of American consumer-buying of automobiles from income-determined to taste-determined market-segmentation – no statistical study could possibly have shown. By the time this could be captured in numbers, it was too late – the Edsel had been brought out and had failed.

The truly important events on the outside are not the trends. They are changes in the trends. These determine ultimately success or failure of an organization and its efforts. Such changes, however, have to be perceived; they cannot be counted, defined or classified. The classifications still produce the expected figures – as they did for the Edsel. But the figures no longer correspond to actual behaviour.

The computer is a logic machine, and that is its strength – but also its limitation. The important events on the outside cannot be reported in the kind of form a computer (or any other logic system) could possibly handle. Man, however, while not particularly logical is perceptive – and that is his strength.

The danger is that executives will become contemptuous of information and stimulus that cannot be reduced to computer logic and computer language. Executives may become blind to everything that is perception, i.e. event, rather than fact, i.e. after the event. The tremendous amount of computer information may thus shut out access to reality.

Eventually the computer – potentially by far the most useful management tool – should make executives aware of their insulation and free them up for more time on the outside. In the short run, however, there is danger of acute 'computeritis'. It is a serious affliction.

The computer only makes acute a condition that existed before it. Executives of necessity live and work within an organization. Unless they make conscious efforts to perceive the outside, the inside may blind them to the true reality.

These four realities the executive cannot change. They are necessary conditions of his existence. But he must therefore assume that he will be ineffectual unless he makes special efforts to learn to be effective.

IV. The Promise of Effectiveness

Increasing effectiveness may well be the only area where we can hope significantly to raise the level of executive performance, achievement, and satisfaction.

We certainly could use people of much greater abilities in many places. We could use people of broader knowledge. I submit, however, that in these two areas, not too much can be expected from further efforts. We may be getting to the point where we are already attempting to do the inherently impossible or at least the inherently unprofitable. But we are not going to breed a new race of supermen. We will have to run our organizations with men as they are.

The books on manager development for instance envisage truly a 'man for all seasons' in their picture of 'the manager of to-morrow'. A senior executive, we are told, should have extraordinary abilities as an analyst and as a decision-maker. He should be good at working with people and at understanding organization and power relations, good at mathematics and have artistic insight and creative imagination. What seems to be wanted is universal genius; and universal genius has always been in scarce supply. The experience of the human race indicates strongly that the only person in abundant supply is the universal incompetent. We will therefore have to staff our organizations with people who at best excel in one of these abilities. And then they are more than likely to lack any but the most modest endowment in the others.

We will have to learn to build organizations in such a manner that any man who has strength in one important area is capable of putting it to work (as will be discussed in considerable depth in

Chapter 4 below). But we cannot expect to get the executive performance we need by raising our standards for abilities, let alone by hoping for the universally gifted man. We will have to extend the range of human beings through the tools they have to work with rather than through a sudden quantum jump in human ability.

The same, more or less, applies to knowledge. However badly we may need people of more and better knowledge, the effort needed to make a major improvement may well be greater than any possible, let alone any probable, return.

> Fifteen years ago when operational research first came in, several of the brilliant young practitioners published their prescription for the operational-researcher of tomorrow. They always came out asking for a polymath knowing everything and capable of doing superior and original work in every area of human knowledge. According to one of these studies, operational-researchers need to have advanced knowledge in sixty-two or so major scientific and humanistic disciplines. If such a man could be found, he would, I am afraid, be totally wasted on studies of inventory levels or on the programming of production schedules.

Much less ambitious programmes for manager development call for high knowledge in such a host of divergent skills as accounting and personnel, marketing, pricing, and economic analysis, the behavioural sciences such as psychology, and the natural sciences from physics to biology and geology. And we surely need men who understand the dynamics of modern technology, the complexity of the modern world economy, and the labyrinth of modern government.

Every one of these is a big area, too big, indeed, even for men who work on nothing else. The scholars tend to specialize in fairly small segments of each of these fields and do not pretend to have more than a journeyman's knowledge of the field itself.

I am not saying that one need not try to understand the fundamentals of every one of these areas.

> One of the weaknesses of young, highly educated people today – whether in business, medicine or government – is that they are satisfied to be versed in one narrow speciality and affect a contempt for the other areas. One need not know in detail what to do with 'human relations' as an accountant, or how to promote a new branded product if an engineer. But one

has a responsibility to know at least what these areas are about, why they are around, and what they are trying to do. One need not know psychiatry to be a good urologist. But one had better know what psychiatry is all about. One need not be an international lawyer to do a good job in the Department of Agriculture. But one had better know enough about international politics not to do international damage through a parochial farm policy.

This, however, is something very different from the universal expert – who is as unlikely to occur as the universal genius. Instead we will have to learn how to make better use of people who are good in any one of these areas. But this means increasing effectiveness. If one cannot increase the supply of a resource, one must increase its yield. And effectiveness is the one tool to make the resources of ability and knowledge yield more and better results.

Effectiveness thus deserves high priority because of the needs of organization. It deserves even greater priority as the tool of the executive and as his access to achievement and performance.

V. But Can Effectiveness Be Learned?

If effectiveness were a gift people were born with, the way they are born with a gift for music or an eye for painting, we would be in bad shape. For we know that only a small minority is born with great gifts in any one of these areas. We would therefore be reduced to trying to spot people with high potential of effectiveness early and to train them as best we know to develop their talent. But we could hardly hope to find enough people for the executive tasks of modern society this way. Indeed, if effectiveness were a gift, our present civilization would be highly vulnerable, if not untenable. As a civilization of large organizations it is dependent on a large supply of people capable of being executives with a modicum of effectiveness.

If effectiveness can be learned, however, the questions arise: What does it consist in? What does one have to learn? Of what kind is the learning? Is it a knowledge – and knowledge one learns in systematic form and through concepts? Is it a skill which one learns as an apprentice? Or is it a practice which one learns through doing the same elementary things over and over again?

I have been asking this question for a good many years. As a consultant, I work with executives in many organizations. Effectiveness is crucial to me in two ways. First, a consultant who by definition has no authority other than that of knowledge, must himself be effective – or else he is nothing. Even the most effective consultant depends on people within the client organization to get anything done. Their effectiveness therefore determines in the last analysis whether a consultant contributes and achieves results, or whether he is pure 'cost centre' or at best a court jester.

I soon learned that there is no 'effective personality'.* The effective executives I have seen differ widely in their temperaments and their abilities, in what they do and how they do it, in their personalities, their knowledge, their interests – in fact in almost everything that distinguishes human beings. All they have in common is the ability to get the right things done.

Among the effective executives I have known and worked with, there are extroverts and aloof, retiring men, some even morbidly shy. Some are eccentrics, others painfully correct conformists. Some are fat and some are lean. Some are worriers, some are relaxed. Some drink quite heavily, others are total abstainers. Some are men of great charm and warmth, some have no more personality than a frozen mackerel. There are a few men among them who would answer to the popular conception of a 'leader'. But equally there are colourless men who would attract no attention in a crowd. Some are scholars and serious students, others almost unlettered. Some have broad interests, others know nothing except their own narrow area and care for little else. Some of the men are self-centred, if not indeed selfish. But there are also some who are generous of heart and mind. There are men who live only for their work and others whose main interests lie outside – in community work, in their church, in the study of Chinese poetry,

* As is asserted in an unpublished (and undated) talk which Professor Chris Argyris of Yale University made at the Graduate Business School of Columbia University. According to Professor Argyris, the 'successful' executive (as he calls him) has ten characteristics, among them 'High Frustration Tolerance', understanding of the 'Laws of Competitive Warfare', or that he 'Identifies with Groups'. If this were indeed the executive personality we need, we would be in real trouble. There are not too many people around with such personality traits, and no one has ever known a way of acquiring them. Fortunately, I know many highly effective – and successful – executives who lack most, if not all, of Argyris's 'characteristics'. I also know quite a few who, though they answer Argyris's description, are singularly ineffectual.

or in modern music. Among the effective executives I have met, there are people who use logic and analysis and others who rely mainly on perception and intuition. There are men who make decisions easily and men who suffer agonies every time they have to move.

Effective executives, in other words, differ as widely as physicians, high-school teachers, or violinists. They differ as widely as do ineffectual ones, are indeed indistinguisable from ineffectual executives in type, personality, and talents.

What all these effective executives have in common is the practices that make effective whatever they have and whatever they are. And these practices are the same, whether the effective executive works in a business or in a government agency, as hospital administrator or as university dean.

But whenever I have found a man, no matter how great his intelligence, his industry, his imagination, or his knowledge, who failed to observe these practices, I have also found an executive deficient in effectiveness.

Effectiveness, in other words is a habit, that is a complex of practices. And practices can always be learned. Practices are simple, deceptively so; even a seven-year-old has no difficulty in understanding a practice. But practices are always exceedingly hard to do well. They have to be acquired as we all learned the multiplication table, that is, repeated *ad nauseam* until '$6 \times 6 = 36$' has become an unthinking, conditioned reflex and a firmly ingrained habit. Practices one learns by practising and practising and practising again.

To every practice applies what my old piano teacher said to me in exasperation when I was a small boy. 'You will never play Mozart the way Arthur Schnabel does, but there is no reason in the world why you should not play your scales the way he does.' What the piano teacher forgot to add – probably because it was so patently obvious to her – is that even the great pianists could not play Mozart as they do, unless they practised their scales and kept on practising them.

There is, in other words, no reason why anyone with normal endowment should not acquire competency in any practice. Mastery might well elude him; for this one might need special talents. But what is needed in effectiveness is competency. What is needed are 'the scales'.

There are essentially five such practices – five such habits of the mind that have to be acquired to be an effective executive.

1. Effective executives know where their time goes. They work systematically at managing the little of their time that can be brought under their control.

2. Effective executives focus on outward contribution. They gear their efforts to results rather than to work. They start out with the question, 'What results are expected of me?' rather than with the work to be done, let alone with its techniques and tools.

3. Effective executives build on strengths – their own strengths, the strengths of their superiors, colleagues, and subordinates; and on the strengths in the situation, that is, on what they can do. They do not build on weakness. They do not start out with the things they can't do.

4. Effective executives concentrate on the few major areas where superior performance will produce outstanding results. They force themselves to set priorities and stay with their priority decisions. They know that they have no choice but to do first things first and second things not at all. The alternative is to get nothing done.

5. Effective executives finally make effective decisions. They know that this is, above all, a matter of system – of the right steps in the right sequence. They know that an effective decision is always a judgment, based on 'dissenting opinions' rather than on 'consensus on the facts'. And they know that to make many decisions fast means to make the wrong decisions. What is needed are few, but fundamental, decisions. What is needed is the right strategy rather than razzle-dazzle tactics.

These are the elements of executive effectiveness – and these are the subjects of this book.

2

Know Thy Time

Most discussions of the executive's task start with the advice to plan one's work. This sounds eminently plausible. The only thing wrong with it is that it rarely works. The plans always remain on paper, always remain good intentions. They seldom turn into achievement.

Effective executives, in my observation, do not start with their tasks. They start with their time. And they do not start out with planning. They start by finding out where their time actually goes. Then they attempt to manage their time and to cut back unproductive demands on their time. Finally they consolidate their 'discretionary' time into the largest possible continuing units. This three-step process:

- recording time;
- managing time; and
- consolidating time

is the foundation of executive effectiveness.

Effective executives know that time is the limiting factor. The output limits of any process are set by the scarcest resource. In the process we call 'accomplishment', this is time.

Time is also a unique resource. Of the other major resources, money is actually quite plentiful. We long ago should have learned that it is the demand for capital, rather than the supply thereof, which sets the limit to economic growth and activity. People – the third limiting resource – one can hire, though one can rarely hire enough good people. But one cannot rent, hire, buy, or otherwise obtain more time.

The supply of time is totally inelastic. No matter how high the demand, the supply will not go up. There is no price for it and no marginal utility curve for it. Moreover, time is totally perishable and cannot be stored. Yesterday's time is gone for ever and will never come back. Time is, therefore, always in exceedingly short supply.

Time is totally irreplaceable. Within limits we can substitute one resource for another, copper for aluminium, for instance. We can substitute capital for human labour. We can use more knowledge or more brawn. But there is no substitute for time.

Everything requires time. It is the one truly universal condition. All work takes place in time and uses up time. Yet most people take for granted this unique, irreplaceable, and necessary resource. Nothing else, perhaps, distinguishes effective executives as much as their tender loving care of time.

Man is ill-equipped to manage his time.

Though man, like all living beings, has a 'biological clock' – as anyone discovers who crosses the Atlantic by jet – he lacks, as psychological experiments have shown, a reliable time sense. People kept in a room in which they cannot see light and darkness outside rapidly lose all sense of time. Even in total darkness, most people retain their sense of space. But even with the lights on, a few hours in a sealed room make most people incapable of estimating how much time has elapsed. They are as likely grossly to underrate the time spent in the room as grossly to overrate it.

If we rely on our memory, therefore, we do not know how time has been spent.

I sometimes ask executives who pride themselves on their memory to put down their guess as to how they spend their own time. Then I lock these guesses away for a few weeks or months. In the meantime, the executives run an actual time record on themselves. There is never much resemblance between the way these men thought they used their time and their actual records.

One company chairman was absolutely certain that he divided his time roughly into three parts. One third he thought he was spending with his senior men. One third he thought he spent with his important customers. And one third he thought was devoted to community activities. The actual record of his activities over six weeks brought out clearly that he spent almost no time in any of these areas. These were the tasks on which he knew he *should* spend time – and therefore memory, obliging as usual, told him that these were the tasks on which he actually had spent his time. The record showed, however, that he spent most of his hours as a kind of dispatcher, keeping track of orders from customers he personally knew and bothering the plant with telephone calls about them. Most of these orders were going through all right anyhow and his intervention could only delay them. But when his secretary first came in with the time record he did not believe her. It took two or three more time logs to convince him that record, rather than memory, has to be trusted when it comes to the use of time.

The effective executive therefore knows that to manage his time, he first has to know where it actually goes.

I. The Time Demands on the Executive

There are constant pressures toward unproductive and wasteful time use. Any executive, whether he is a manager or not, has to spend a great deal of his time on things that do not contribute at all. Much is inevitably wasted. The higher up in the organization he is, the more demands on his time will the organization make.

The head of a large company once told me that in two years as chief executive officer he had 'eaten out' every evening except on Christmas Day and New Year's Day. All the other dinners were 'official' functions, each of which wasted several hours. Yet he saw no possible alternative. Whether the dinner honoured an employee retiring after fifty years of service, or the governor of one of the states in which the company did business, the chief executive officer had to be there. Ceremony is one of his tasks. My friend had no illusions that these dinners contributed anything either to the company or to his own entertainment or self-development. Yet he had to be there and dine graciously.

Similar time-wasters abound in the life of every executive. When a company's best customer calls up, the sales manager cannot say 'I am busy.' He has to listen, even though all the customer wants to talk about may be a bridge game the preceding Saturday or the chances of his daughter's getting into the right college. The hospital administrator has to attend the meetings of every one of his staff committees, or else the physicians, the nurses, the technicians and so on feel that they are being slighted. The government administrator had better pay attention when a Congressman calls and wants some information he could, in less time, get out of the telephone book or the *World Almanac*. And so it goes all day long.

Non-managers are no better off. They too are bombarded with demands on their time which add little, if anything, to their productivity, and yet cannot be disregarded.

In every executive job, a large part of the time must therefore be wasted on things which, though they apparently have to be done, contribute nothing or little.

Yet most of the tasks of the executive require, for minimum effectiveness, a fairly large quantum of time. To spend in one stretch less than this minimum is sheer waste. One accomplishes nothing and has to begin all over again.

To write a report may, for instance, require six or eight hours, at least for the first draft. It is pointless to give seven hours to the task by spending fifteen minutes twice a day for three weeks. All one has at the end is blank paper with some doodles on it. But if one can lock the door, disconnect the telephone, and sit down to wrestle with the report for five or six hours without interruption, one has a good chance to come up with what I call a 'zero draft' – the one before the first draft. From then on, one can indeed work in fairly small instalments, can rewrite, correct and edit section by section, paragraph by paragraph, sentence by sentence.

The same goes for an experiment. One simply has to have five to twelve hours in a single stretch to set up the apparatus and to do at least one completed run. Or one has to start all over again after an interruption.

To be effective, every knowledge worker, and especially every executive, therefore needs to be able to dispose of time in fairly large chunks. To have small dibs and dabs of time at his disposal will not be sufficient even if the total is an impressive number of hours.

This is particularly true with respect to time spent working with people, which is, of course, a central task in the work of the executive. People are time-consumers. And most people are time-wasters.

To spend a few minutes with people is simply not productive. If one wants to get anything across, one has to spend a fairly large minimum quantum of time. The manager who thinks that he can discuss the plans, direction, and performance of one of his subordinates in fifteen minutes – and many managers believe this – is just deceiving himself. If one wants to get to the point of having an impact, one needs probably at least an hour and usually much more. And if one has to establish a human relationship, one needs infinitely more time.

Relations with other knowledge workers are especially time-consuming. Whatever the reason – whether it is the absence of the barrier of class and authority between superior and subordinate in knowledge work, or whether he simply takes himself more seriously – the knowledge worker makes much greater time demands than the manual worker on his superior as well as on his associates. Moreover, because knowledge work cannot be measured the way manual work can, one cannot tell a knowledge worker in a few simple words whether he is doing the right job and how well he is doing it. One can say to a manual worker, 'our work standard calls for fifty pieces an hour, and you are only turning out forty-two'. One has to sit down with a knowledge worker and think through with him what should be done and why, before one can even know whether he is doing a satisfactory job or not. And this is time-consuming.

Since the knowledge worker directs himself, he must understand what achievement is expected of him and why. He must also understand the work of the people who have to use his knowledge output. For this, he needs a good deal of information, discussion, instruction – all things that take time. And contrary to common belief, this time demand is made not only on his superior but equally on his colleagues.

The knowledge worker must be focused on the results and performance goals of the entire organization to have any results and performance at all. This means that he has to set aside time to direct his vision from his work to results, and from his speciality to the outside in which alone performance lies.

Wherever knowledge workers perform well in large organizations, senior executives take time out, on a regular schedule, to sit down with them sometimes all the way down to green juniors, and ask: 'What should we at the head of this organization know about your work? What do you want to tell me regarding this organization? Where do you see opportunities we do not exploit? Where do you see dangers to which we are still blind? And, altogether, what do you want to know from me about the organization?'

This leisurely exchange is needed equally in a government agency and in a business, in a research lab and in an army staff. Without it, the knowledge people either lose enthusiasm and become time-servers, or they direct their energies toward their speciality and away from the opportunities and needs of the organization. But such a session takes a great deal of time, especially as it should be unhurried and relaxed. People must feel that 'we have all the time in the world'. This actually means that one gets a great deal done fast. But it means also that one has to make available a good deal of time in one chunk and without too much interruption.

Mixing personal relations and work relations is time-consuming. If hurried, it turns into friction. Yet any organization rests on this mixture. The more people are together, the more time will their sheer interaction take, the less time will be available to them for work, accomplishment, and results.

Management literature has long known the theorem of 'the span of control' which asserts that one man can manage only a few people if these people have to come together in their own work (that is, for instance, an accountant, a sales manager, and a manufacturing man, all three of whom have to work with each other to get any results). On the other hand, managers of chain stores in different cities do not have to work with each other, so that any number could conceivably report to one regional vice-president without violating the principle of the 'span of control'. Whether this theorem is valid or not, there is little doubt that the more people have to work together, the more time will be spent on 'interacting' rather than on work and accomplishment. Large organization creates strength by lavishly using the executive's time.

The larger the organization, therefore, the less actual time will the executive have. The more important will it be for him to know where his time goes and to manage the little time at his disposal.

The more people there are in an organization, the more often does a decision on people arise. But fast personnel decisions are likely to be wrong decisions. The time quantum of the good personnel decision is amazingly large. What the decision involves often becomes clear only when one has gone around the same track several times.

Among the effective executives I have had occasion to observe, there have been people who make decisions fast, and people who make them rather slowly. But without exception, they make personnel decisions slowly and they make them several times before they really commit themselves.

Alfred P. Sloan, Jr., former head of General Motors, the

world's largest manufacturing company, was reported never to make a personnel decision the first time it came up. He made a tentative judgment, and even that took several hours as a rule. Then, a few days or weeks later, he tackled the question again, as if he had never worked on it before. Only when he came up with the same name two or three times in a row was he willing to go ahead. Sloan had a deserved reputation for the 'winners' he picked. But when asked about his secret, he is reported to have said: 'No secret – I have simply accepted that the first name I come up with is likely to be the wrong name – and I therefore retrace the whole process of thought and analysis a few times before I act.' Yet Sloan was far from a patient man.

Few executives make personnel decisions of such impact. But all effective executives I have had occasion to observe have learned that they have to give several hours of continuous and uninterrupted thought to decisions on people if they hope to come up with the right answer.

The director of a medium-sized government research institute found this out when one of his senior administrators had to be removed from his job. The man was in his fifties and had been with the institute all his working life. After years of good work, the man suddenly began to deteriorate. He clearly could no longer handle his job. But even if civil service rules had permitted it, the man could not be fired. He could of course have been demoted. But this, the director felt, would destroy the man – and the institute owed him consideration and loyalty for years of productive, loyal service. Yet he could not be kept in an administrative position; his shortcomings were much too obvious and were, indeed, weakening the whole institute.

The director and his deputy had been over this situation many times without seeing a way out. But when they sat down for a quiet evening where they could give three or four hours uninterruptedly to the problem, the 'obvious' solution finally emerged. It was indeed so simple that neither could explain why he had not seen it before. It got the man out of the wrong job into a job which needed being done and which yet did not require the administrative performance he was no longer able to give.

Time in large, continuous, and uninterrupted units is needed for such decisions as whom to put on a task force set up to study a specific problem; what responsibilities to entrust to the manager of a new organizational unit or to the new manager of an old organizational unit; whether to promote into a vacancy a man who has the marketing knowledge needed for the job but lacks technical training, or whether to put in a first-rate technical man without much marketing background, and so on.

People-decisions are time-consuming, for the simple reason that the Good Lord did not create people as 'resources' for organization. They do not come in the proper size and shape for the tasks that have to be done in organization – and they cannot be machined down or re-cast for these tasks. People are always 'almost fits' at best. To get the work done with people (and no other resource is available) therefore requires lots of time, thought, and judgment.

The Slavic peasant of Eastern Europe used to have a proverb, 'What one does not have in one's feet, one's got to have in one's head.' This may be considered a fanciful version of the law of the conservation of energy. But it is above all something like a 'law of the conservation of time'. The more time we take out of the task of the 'legs' – that is of physical, manual-work, the more will we have to spend on the work of the 'head' – that is on knowledge work. The easier we make it for rank and file workers, machine tenders as well as clerks, the more will have to be done by the knowledge worker. One cannot 'take knowledge out of the work'. It has to be put back somewhere – and in much larger and cohesive amounts.

Time demands on the knowledge worker are not going down. Machine tenders now work only forty hours a week – and soon may work only thirty-five and live better than anybody ever lived before, no matter how much he worked or how rich he was. But the machine tender's leisure is inescapably being paid for by the knowledge worker's longer hours. It is not the executives who have a problem of spending their leisure time in the industrial countries of the world today. On the contrary, they are working everywhere longer hours and have greater demands on their time to satisfy. And the executive time scarcity is bound to become worse rather than better.

One important reason for this is that a high standard of living presupposes an economy of innovation and change. But innovation and change make inordinate time demands on the executive. All one can think and do in a short time is to think what one already knows and to do as one has always done.

There has been an enormous amount of discussion lately to explain why the British economy has lagged so badly since World War II. One of the reasons is surely that the British businessman of the older generation tried to have it as easy as his workers and to work the same short hours. But this is possible only if the business or the industry clings to the old established routine and shuns innovation and change.

For all these reasons, the demands of the organization, the demands of people, the time demands of change and innovation, it will become increasingly important for executives to be able to manage their time. But one cannot even think of managing one's time unless one first knows where it goes.

II. Time Diagnosis

That one has to record time before one can know where it goes and before, in turn, one can attempt to manage it we have realized for the best part of a century. That is, we have known this in respect to manual work, skilled and unskilled, since Scientific Management around 1900 began to record the time it takes for a specific piece of manual work to be done. Hardly any country is today so far behind in industrial methods as not to time systematically the operations of manual workers.

We have applied this knowledge for the work where time does not greatly matter, that is where the difference between time use and time waste is primarily efficiency and costs. But we have not applied it to the work that matters increasingly, and that particularly has to cope with time: the work of the knowledge worker and especially of the executive. Here the difference between time use and time waste is effectiveness and results.

The first step toward executive effectiveness is therefore to record actual time use.

The specific method in which the record is put together need not concern us here. There are executives who keep such a time log themselves. Others, such as the company chairman last mentioned, have their secretaries do it for them. The important thing is that it gets done, and that the record is made in 'real' time, that is at the time of the event itself, rather than later on from memory.

A good many effective executives keep such a log continuously and look at it regularly every month. At a minimum, effective executives have the log run on themselves for three to four weeks at a stretch twice a year or so on a regular schedule. After each such sample, they re-think and re-work their schedule. But six months later, they invariably find that they have 'drifted' into wasting their time on trivia. Time use does improve with practice. But only constant efforts at managing time can prevent drifting.

Systematic time management is therefore the next step. One has to find the non-productive, time-wasting activities and get rid of them if one possibly can. This requires asking oneself a number of diagnostic questions.

1. First one tries to identify and eliminate the things that need not be done at all, the things that are purely waste of time without any results whatever. To find these time-wastes, one asks of *all* activities in the time records: 'What would happen if this were not done at all?' And if the answer is, 'Nothing would happen,' then obviously the conclusion is to stop doing it.

It is amazing how many things busy people are doing that never will be missed. There are, for instance, the countless speeches, dinners, committee memberships, and directorships which take an unconscionable toll of the time of very busy people, which are rarely enjoyed by them or done well by them, but which are endured, year in and year out as an Egyptian Plague ordained from on high. Actually, all one has to do is to learn to say 'no' if an activity contributes nothing to one's own organization, to oneself, or to the organization for which it is to be performed.

The chief executive mentioned above who had to dine out every night found when he analysed these dinners, that at least one third would proceed just as well without anyone from the company's senior management. In fact, he found (somewhat to his chagrin) that his acceptance of a good many of these invitations was by no means welcome to his hosts. They had invited him as a polite gesture. But they had fully expected to be turned down and did not quite know what to do with him when he accepted.

I have yet to see an executive, regardless of rank or station, who could not consign something like a quarter of the demands on his time to the wastepaper basket without anybody noticing their disappearance.

2. The next question is: 'Which of the activities on my time log could be done by somebody else just as well, if not better?'

The dinner-eating company chairman found that any senior executive of the company would do for another third of the formal dinners – all the occasion demanded was the company's name on the guest list.

There has been for years a great deal of talk about 'delegation' in management. Every manager whatever the organization – business, government, university, or armed service – has been exhorted to be a better 'delegator'. In fact, most managers in large organizations have themselves given this sermon and more than once.

I have yet to see any results from all this preaching. The reason why no one listens is simple: as usually presented, delegation makes little sense. If it means that somebody else ought to do part of '*my* work', it is wrong. One is paid for doing one's own work. And if it implies, as the usual sermon does, that the laziest manager is the best manager, it is not only nonsense; it is immoral.

But I have never seen an executive confronted with his time record who did not rapidly acquire the habit of pushing at other people everything that he need not do personally. The first look at the time record makes it abundantly clear that there just is not time enough to do the things the executive himself considers important, himself wants to do, and is himself committed to doing. The only way he can get to the important things is by pushing on others anything that can be done by them at all.

A good example is executive travel. Professor C. Northcote Parkinson has pointed out in one of his delightful satires that the quickest way to get rid of an inconvenient superior is to make a world traveller out of him. The jet plane is indeed overrated as a management tool. A great many trips have to be made; but a junior can make most of them. Travel is still a novelty for him. He is still young enough to get a good night's rest in hotel beds. The junior can take the fatigue – and he will therefore also do a better job than the more experienced, perhaps better trained, but tired superior.

There are also the meetings one attends, even though nothing is going to happen that someone else could not handle. There are the hours spent discussing a document before there is even a first draft that can be discussed. There is, in the research lab, the time spent by a senior physicist to write a 'popular' news release on some of his work. Yet there are plenty of people around with enough science to understand what the physicist is trying to say, who can write readable English where the physicist only speaks higher mathematics. Altogether, an enormous amount of the work being done by executives is work that can easily be done by others, and therefore should be done by others.

'Delegation' as the term is customarily used, is a misunderstanding—is indeed mis-direction. But getting rid of anything that can be done by somebody else so that one does not have to delegate but can really get to one's own work – that is a major improvement in effectiveness.

3. A common cause of time waste is largely under the executive's control and can be eliminated by him. That is the time of others he himself wastes.

There is no one symptom for this. But there is still a simple way to find out. That is to ask other people. Effective executives have learned to ask systematically and without coyness: 'What do I do that wastes your time without contributing to your effectiveness?' To ask this question, and to ask it without being afraid of the truth is, therefore, a mark of the effective executive.

The manner in which an executive does productive work may still be a major waste of somebody else's time.

The senior financial executive of a large organization knew perfectly well that the meetings in his office wasted a lot of time. This man asked all his direct subordinates to every meeting, whatever the topic. As a result the meetings were far too large. And because every participant felt that he had to show interest, everybody asked at least one question – most of them irrelevant. As a result the meetings stretched on endlessly. But the senior executive had not known, until he asked, that his subordinates too considered the meetings a waste of their time. Aware of the great importance everyone in the organization placed on status and on being 'in the know', he had feared that the uninvited men would feel slighted and left out. Now he satisfies the status-needs of his subordinates in a different manner. He sends out a printed form which reads: 'I have asked (Messrs Smith, Jones, and Robinson) to meet with me (Wednesday at 3) in (the fourth floor conference-room) to discuss (next year's capital appropriations budget). Please come if you think that you need the information or want to take part in the discussion. But you will in any event receive right away a full summary of the discussion and of any decisions reached, together with a request for your comments.'

Where formerly a dozen people came and stayed all afternoon, three men and a secretary to take the notes now get the matter over within an hour or so. And no one feels left out.

Many executives know all about these unproductive and unnecessary time demands; yet they are afraid to prune them. They are afraid to cut out something important by mistake. But this mistake, if made, can be speedily corrected. If one prunes too harshly, one usually finds out fast enough.

Every new President of the United States accepts too many invitations at first. Then it dawns on him that he has other work to do and that most of these invitations do not add to his effectiveness. Thereupon, he usually cuts back too sharply and becomes inaccessible. A few weeks or months later, however, he is being told by the press and the radio that he is 'losing touch'. Then he usually finds the right balance between being exploited without effectiveness and using public appearances as his national pulpit.

In fact, there is not much risk that an executive will cut back too much. We usually tend to overrate rather than underrate our importance and to conclude that far too many things can only be done by ourselves. Even very effective executives still do a great many unnecessary, unproductive things.

But the best proof that the danger of over-pruning is a bugaboo is the extraordinary effectiveness so often attained by severely ill or severely handicapped people.

A good example was Harry Hopkins, President Roosevelt's confidential adviser in World War II. A dying, indeed almost a dead man for whom every step was torment, he could only work a few hours every other day or so. This forced him to cut out everything but truly vital matters. He did not lose effectiveness thereby; on the contrary, he became as Churchill called him,

'Lord of the Heart of the Matter' and accomplished more than anyone else in wartime Washington.

This is an extreme, of course. But it illustrates both how much control one can exercise over one's time if one really tries, and how much of the time-wasters one can cut out without loss of effectiveness.

III. Pruning the Time-wasters

These three diagnostic questions deal with unproductive and time-consuming activities over which every executive has some control. Every knowledge worker and every executive should ask them. Managers, however, need to be equally concerned with time-loss that results from poor management and deficient organization. Poor management wastes everybody's time – but above all, it wastes the manager's time.

1. The first task here is to identify the time-wasters which follow from lack of system or foresight. The symptom to look for is the recurrent 'crisis', the crisis that comes back year after year. A crisis that recurs a second time is a crisis that must not occur again.

The annual inventory crisis belongs here. That with the computer we now can meet it even more 'heroically' and at greater expense than we could in the past is hardly a great improvement.

A recurrent crisis should always have been foreseen. It can therefore either be prevented or reduced to a routine which clerks can manage. The definition of a 'routine' is that it makes unskilled people without judgment capable of doing what it took near-genius to do before; for a routine puts down in systematic, step-by-step form what a very able man learned in surmounting yesterday's crisis.

The recurrent crisis is not confined to the lower levels of an organization. It afflicts everyone.

For years, a fairly large company ran into one of these crises annually around the first of December. In a highly seasonal business, with the last quarter usually the year's low, fourth-quarter sales and profits were not easily predictable. Every year, however, management made an earnings prediction when it issued its interim report at the end of the second quarter. Three months later, in the fourth quarter, there was tremendous scurrying and company-wide emergency action to live up to top management's forecast. For three to five weeks, nobody in the management group got any work done. It took only one stroke of the pen to solve this crisis; instead of predicting a definite year-end figure, top management is now predicting results within a range. This fully satisfies directors, stockholders, and the financial community. And what used to be a crisis a few years ago, now is no longer even noticed in the company – yet fourth-quarter results are quite a bit better than they used to be, since executive time is no longer being wasted on making results fit the forecast.

Prior to Mr McNamara's appointment as Secretary of Defence, a similar last-minute crisis shook the entire American defence establishment every Spring – toward the end of the fiscal year on 30 June. Every manager in the defence establishment, military or civilian, tried desperately in May and June to find expenditures for the money appropriated by Congress for the fiscal year. Otherwise, he was afraid he would have to give back the money. (This last-minute spending spree has also been a chronic disease in Russian planning.) And yet, this crisis was totally unnecessary as Mr McNamara immediately saw. The law had always permitted the placing of unspent, but needed, sums into an interim account.

The recurrent crisis is simply a symptom of slovenliness and laziness.

Years ago when I first started out as a consultant, I had to learn how to tell a well-managed industrial plant from a poorly managed one – without any pretence to production knowledge. A well-managed plant, I soon learned, is a quiet place. A factory that is 'dramatic', a factory in which the 'epic of industry' is unfolded before the visitor's eyes, is poorly managed. A well-managed factory is boring. Nothing exciting happens in it because the crises have been anticipated and have been converted into routine.

Similarly a well-managed organization is a 'dull' organization. The 'dramatic' things in such an organization are basic decisions that make the future, rather than heroics in mopping up yesterday.

2. Time-wastes often result from overstaffing.

My first-grade arithmetic primer asked: 'If it takes two ditch-diggers two days to dig a ditch, how long would it take four ditch-diggers?' In first grade, the correct answer is, of course, 'one day'. In the kind of work, however, with which executives are concerned, the right answer is probably 'four days' if not 'forever'.

A work force may, indeed, be too small for the task. And the work then suffers, if it gets done at all. But this is not the rule. Much more common is the work force that is too big for effectiveness, the work force that spends, therefore, an increasing amount of its time 'interacting' rather than working.

There is a fairly reliable sympton of overstaffing. If the senior people in the group – and of course the manager in particular – spend more than a small fraction of their time, maybe one tenth, on problems of human relations, on feuds and frictions, on jurisdictional disputes and questions of cooperation, and so on, then the work force is almost certainly too large. People get into each other's way. People have become an impediment to performance, rather than the means thereto. In a lean organization people have room to move without colliding with one another and can do their work without having to explain it all the time.

The excuse for overstaffing is always 'but we have to have a thermodynamicist (or a patent lawyer, or an economist) on the staff'. This specialist is not being used much; he may not be used at all; but 'we have to have him around just in case we need him'. (And he always 'has to be familiar with our problem' and 'be part of the group from the start'!) One should only have on a team the knowledges and skills that are needed day in and day out for the bulk of the work. Specialists that may be needed once in a while, or that may have to be consulted on this or on that, should always remain outside.

It is infinitely cheaper to go to them and consult them against a fee than to have them in the group – to say nothing of the impact an under-employed but overskilled man has on the effectiveness of the entire group. All he can do is mischief.

3. Another common time-waster is malorganization. Its symptom is an excess of meetings.

Meetings are by definition a concession to deficient organization.

For one either meets or one works. One cannot do both at the same time. In an ideally designed structure (which in a changing world is of course only a dream) there would be no meetings. Everybody would know what he needs to know to do his job. Everyone would have the resources available to him to do his job. We meet because people holding different jobs have to cooperate to get a specific task done. We meet because the knowledge and experience needed in a specific situation are not available in one head, but have to be pieced together out of the experience and knowledge of several people.

There will always be more than enough meetings. Organization will always require so much working together that the attempts of well-meaning behavioural scientists to create opportunities for 'cooperation' may be somewhat redundant. But if executives in an organization spend more than a fairly small part of their time in meeting, it is a sure sign of malorganization.

Every meeting generates a host of little follow-up meetings – some formal, some informal, but both stretching out for hours. Meetings, therefore, need to be purposefully directed. An undirected meeting is not just a nuisance; it is a danger. But above all, meetings have to be the exception rather than the rule. An organization in which everybody meets all the time is an organization in which no one gets anything done. Wherever a time log shows the fatty degeneration of meetings – whenever, for instance, people in an organization find themselves in meetings a quarter of their time or more – there is time-wasting malorganization.

> There are exceptions, special organs whose purpose it is to meet – the boards of directors, for instance, of such companies as Du Pont and Standard Oil of New Jersey which are the final organs of deliberation and appeal but which do not operate anything. But as these two companies realized a long time ago, the people who sit on these boards cannot be permitted to do anything else – for the same reason, by the way, that judges cannot be permitted to be also advocates in their spare time.

As a rule, meetings should never be allowed to become the main demand on an executive's time. Too many meetings always bespeak poor structure of jobs and the wrong organizational components. Too many meetings signify that work that should be in one job or in one component is spread over several jobs or several components. They signify that responsibility is diffused and that information is not addressed to the people who need it.

In one large company, the root cause of an epidemic of meetings was a traditional but obsolescent organization of the energy business. Large steam turbines, the company's traditional business since before 1900, were one division under their own management and with their own staff. The company, however, during World War II, also went into aircraft engines and had, as a result, a large jet engine capacity, organized in another division concerned with aircraft and defence production. Finally, there was an atomic energy division, really an offspring of the research labs and still organizationally more or less tied to them.

But today these three power sources are no longer separate, each with its own market. Increasingly, they are becoming substitutes for, as well as complements to, each other. Each of the three is the most economical and most advantageous generating equipment for electric power under certain conditions. In this sense the three are competitive. But by putting two of them together, one can also obtain performance capacities which no one type of equipment by itself possesses.

What the company needed, clearly, was an energy strategy. It needed a decision whether to push all three types of generating equipment, in competition with each other; whether to make one of the three the main business and consider the other two supplementary; or finally, whether to develop two of the three – and which two – as one 'energy package'. It needed a decision how to divide available capital among the three. Above all, however, the energy business needed an organization which expressed the reality of one energy market, producing the same end product, electric power, for the same customers. Instead there were three components, each carefully shielded from the others by layers of organization, each having its own special folkways, rituals, and its own career ladders – and each blithely confident that it would get by itself 75 per cent of the total energy business of the next decade.

As a result, the three were engaged in a non-stop meeting for years. Since each reported to a different member of management, these meetings sucked in the entire top group. Finally, the three were cut loose from their original groups and put together into one organizational component under one manager. There is still a good deal of in-fighting going on; and the big strategy decisions still have to be made. But at least there is understanding now as to what these decisions are. At least top management no longer has to chair and referee every meeting. And total meeting time is a fraction of what it used to be.

4. The last major time-waster is malfunction in information.

The administrator of a large hospital was plagued for years by telephone calls from doctors asking him to find a bed for one of their patients who should be hospitalized. The admissions people 'knew' that there was no empty bed. Yet the administrator almost invariably found a few. The admissions people simply were not informed immediately when a patient was discharged. The floor nurse knew, of course, and so did the people in the front office who presented the bill to the departing patient. The admissions people, however, got a 'bed count', made every morning at 5.00 A.M. – while the great majority of patients were being sent home in mid-morning after the doctors had made the rounds. It did not take genius to put this right; all it needed was an extra carbon copy of the chit that goes from the floor nurse to the front office.

Even worse, but equally common, is information in the wrong form.

Manufacturing businesses typically suffer from production figures that have to be 'translated' before operating people can use them. They report 'averages', that is they report what the accountants need. Operating people, however, usually need not the averages but the range and the extremes – product mix and production fluctuations, length of runs, and so on. To get what they need, they must either spend hours each day adapting the averages or build their own 'secret' accounting organization. The accountant has all the information, but no one, as a rule, had thought of telling him what is needed.

Time-wasting management defects such as overstaffing, malorganization or malfunctioning information can sometimes be remedied fast. At other times, it takes long patient work to correct them. The results of such work are, however, great – and especially in terms of time gained.

IV. Consolidating 'Discretionary Time'

The executive who records and analyses his time and then attempts to manage it, can determine how much he has for his important tasks. How much time is there that is 'discretionary', i.e. available for the big tasks that will really make a contribution?

It is not going to be a great deal no matter how ruthlessly the executive prunes time-wasters.

One of the most accomplished time managers I have ever met was the president of a big bank with whom I worked for two years on top-management structure. I saw him once a month for two years. My appointment was always for an hour and a half. The president was always prepared for the sessions – and I soon learned to do my homework too. There was never more than one item on the agenda. But when I had been in there for an hour and twenty minutes, the president would turn to me and say, 'Mr Drucker, I believe you'd better sum up now and outline what we should do next.' And an hour and thirty minutes after I had been ushered into his office, he was at the door shaking my hand and saying good-bye.

After this had been going on for about one year, I finally asked him, 'Why always an hour and a half?' He answered, 'That's easy. I have found out that my attention span is about an hour and a half. If I work on any one topic longer than this, I begin to repeat myself. At the same time, I have learned that nothing of importance can really be tackled in much less time. One does not get to the point where one understands what one is talking about.'

During the hour and a half I was in his office every month, there was never a telephone call, and his secretary never stuck her head in the door to announce that an important man wanted to see him urgently. One day I asked him about this. He said, 'My secretary has strict instructions not to put anyone through except the President of the United States and my wife. The President rarely calls – and my wife knows better. Everything else the secretary holds till I have finished. Then I have half an hour in which I return every call and make sure I get every message. I have yet to come across a crisis which could not wait ninety minutes.'

Needless to say, this president accomplished more in this onemonthly session than many other and equally able executives get done in a month of meetings.

But even this disciplined man had to resign himself to having at least half his time taken up by things of minor importance and dubious value, things that none the less had to be done – the seeing of important customers who just 'dropped in'; attendance at meetings which could just as well have proceeded without him; specific decisions on daily problems that should not have reached him but invariably did.

Whenever I see a senior executive asserting that more than half his time is under his control, and is really discretionary time which he invests and spends according to his own judgment, I am reasonably certain that he has no idea where his time goes. Senior executives rarely have as much as one quarter of their time truly at their disposal and available for the important matters, the matters that contribute, the matters they are being paid for. This is true in any organization – except that in the government agency the unproductive time demands on the top people tend to be even higher than they are in other large organizations.

The higher up an executive, the larger will be the proportion of time that is not under his control and yet not spent on contribution. The larger the organization, the more time will be needed just to keep the organization together and running, rather than to make it function and produce.

The effective executive therefore knows that he has to consolidate his discretionary time. He knows that he needs large chunks of time and that small driblets are no time at all. Even one quarter of the working day, if consolidated in large time-units, is usually enough to get the important things done. But even three quarters of the working day are useless if they are only available as fifteen minutes here or half an hour there.

The final step in time management is therefore to consolidate the time that record and analysis show as normally available and under the executive's control.

There are a good many ways of doing this. Some people, usually senior men, work at home one day a week; this is a particularly common method of time-consolidation for editors or research scientists.

Other men schedule all the operating work – the meetings, reviews, problem-sessions, and so on – for two days a week, e.g.

Monday and Friday, and set aside the mornings of the remaining days for consistent continuing work on major issues.

> This was how the bank president handled his time. Monday and Friday, he had his operating meetings, saw senior executives on current matters, was available to important customers, and so on. Tuesday, Wednesday, and Thursday afternoons were left unscheduled – for whatever might come up; and something of course always did, whether urgent personnel problems, a surprise visit by one of the bank's representatives from abroad or by an important customer, or a trip to Washington. But in the mornings of these three days he scheduled the work on the major matters – in chunks of ninety minutes each.

Another fairly common method is to schedule a daily work period at home in the morning.

> One of the most effective executives in Professor Sune Carlson's study mentioned above, spent ninety minutes each morning before going to work at home in a study without a telephone. Even if this means working very early so as to get to the office on time, it is preferable to the most popular way of getting to the important work: taking it home in the evening and spending three hours after dinner on it. By that time, most executives are too tired to do a good job. Certainly those of middle age or older are better off going to bed earlier and getting up earlier. And the reason why working home nights is so popular is actually its worst feature: it enables an executive to avoid tackling his time and its management during the day.

But the method by which one consolidates one's discretionary time is far less important than the approach. Most people tackle the job by trying to push the secondary, the less productive matters together, thus clearing, so to speak, a free space between them. This does not lead very far, however. One still gives priority in one's mind and in one's schedule to the less important things, the things that have to be done even though they contribute little. As a result, any new time pressure is likely to be satisfied at the expense of the discretionary time and of the work that should be done in it. Within a few days or weeks, the entire discretionary time will then be gone again, nibbled away by new crises, new immediacies, new trivia.

Effective executives start out by estimating how much discretionary time they can realistically call their own. Then they set aside continuous time in the appropriate amount. And if they find later that other matters encroach on this reserve, they scrutinize their record again and get rid of some more time-demands from less than fully productive activities. They know that, as has been said before, one rarely over-prunes.

And all effective executives control their time-management perpetually. They not only keep a continuing log and analyse it periodically. They set themselves deadlines for the important activities, based on their judgment of their discretionary time. One highly effective man I know, keeps two such lists – one of the urgent and one of the unpleasant things that have to be done – each with a deadline.

When he finds his deadlines slipping, he knows his time is again getting away from him.

Time is the scarcest resource; and unless it is managed, nothing else can be managed. The analysis of one's time, moreover, is the one easily accessible and yet systematic way to analyse one's work and to think through what really matters in it.

'Know Thyself', the old prescription for wisdom, is almost impossibly difficult for mortal men. But everyone can follow the injunction 'Know Thy Time' if he wants to, and be well on the road toward contribution and effectiveness.

3

What Can I Contribute?

The effective executive focuses on contribution. He looks up from his work and outward toward goals. He asks: what can I contribute that will significantly affect the performance and the results of the institution I serve? His stress is on responsibility.

The focus on contribution is the key to effectiveness – in a man's own work, its content, its level, its standards, and its impacts; in his relations with others – his superiors, his associates, his subordinates; in his use of the tools of the executive such as meetings or reports.

The great majority of executives tend to focus downward. They are occupied with efforts rather than with results. They worry over what the organization and their superiors 'owe' them and should do for them. And they are conscious above all of the authority they should have. As a result, they render themselves ineffectual.

The head of one of the large management consulting firms always starts an assignment with a new client by spending a few days visiting the senior executives of the client organization one by one. After he has chatted with them about the assignment and the client organization, its history, and its people, he asks (though rarely, of course, in these words): 'And what do *you* do that justifies your being on the payroll?' The great majority, he reports, answer, 'I run the accounting department.' Or, 'I am in charge of the sales force.' Indeed, not uncommonly, the answer is, 'I have 850 people working under me.' Only a few say, 'It's my job to give our managers the information they need to make the right decisions,' or 'I am responsible for finding out what products the customer will want tomorrow,' or 'I have to think through and prepare the decisions the president will have to face tomorrow.'

The man who focuses on efforts and who stresses his downward authority is a subordinate no matter how exalted his title and rank. But the man who focuses on contribution and who takes responsibility for results no matter how junior, is, in the most literal sense of the phrase, 'top management'. He holds himself accountable for the performance of the whole.

1. The Executive's Own Commitment

The focus on contribution turns the executive's attention away from his own speciality, his own narrow skills, his own department, and toward the performance of the whole. It turns his attention to the outside, the only place where there are results. He is likely to have to think through what relationships his skills, his speciality, his function, or his department have to the entire organization and *its* purpose. He therefore will also come to think in terms of the customer, the client or the patient, who is the ultimate reason for whatever the organization produces, whether it be economic goods, governmental policies or health services. As a result, what he does and how he does it will be materially different.

A large scientific agency of the U.S. Government found this out a few years ago. The old director of publications retired. He had been with the agency since its inception in the thirties and was neither scientist nor trained writer. The publications which he turned out were often criticized for lacking professional polish. He was replaced by an accomplished science writer. The publications immediately took on a highly professional look. But the scientific community for whom these publications were intended stopped reading them. A highly respected university scientist who had for many years worked closely with the agency, finally told the administrator: 'The former director was writing *for* us; your new man writes *at* us.' The old director had asked the question, 'What can I contribute to the results of this agency?' His answer was: 'I can interest the young scientists on the outside in our work, can make them want to come to work for us.' He therefore stressed major problems, major decisions, and even major controversies inside the agency. This had brought him more than once into head-on collision with the administrator. But the old man had stood by his guns. 'The test of our publications is not whether we like them; the test is how many young scientists apply to us for jobs and how good they are,' he said.

To ask: 'What can I contribute?' is to look for the unused potential in the job. And what is considered excellent performance in a good many positions is often but a pale shadow of the job's full potential of contribution.

The Agency department in a large American commercial bank is usually considered a profitable but humdrum activity. This department acts, for a fee, as the registrar and stock-transfer agent for the securities of corporations. It keeps the names of stockholders on record, issues and mails their dividend cheques, and does a host of similar clerical chores – all demanding precision and high efficiency but rarely great imagination.

Or so it seemed until a new agency vice-president in a large New York bank asked the question, 'What could Agency contribute?' He then realized that the work brought him into direct contact with the senior financial executives of the bank's customers who make the 'buying decisions' on all banking services – deposits, loans, investments, pension-fund management, and so on. Of course, the Agency department by itself has to be run efficiently. But as this new vice-president realized, its greatest potential was as a sales force for all the other services of the bank. Under its new head, Agency, formerly an efficient paper-pusher, became a highly successful marketing force for the entire bank.

Executives who do not ask themselves: 'What can I contribute?' are not only likely to aim too low, they are likely to aim at the wrong things. Above all, they may define their contribution too narrowly.

'Contribution', as the two illustrations just given show, may mean different things. For every organization needs performance in three major areas: it needs direct results; building of values and their reaffirmation; and building and developing people for tomorrow. If deprived of performance in any one of these areas, it will decay and die. All three therefore have to be built into the contribution of every executive. But their relative importance varies greatly with the personality and the position of the executive as well as with the needs of the organization.

The direct results of an organization are clearly visible, as a rule. In a business, they are economic results, such as sales and profits. In a hospital, they are patient care, and so on. But even direct results are not totally unambiguous as the example of the Agency vice-president in the bank illustrates. And when there is confusion as to what they should be, there are no results. One example is the performance (or rather lack of performance) of the nationalized airlines of Great Britain. They are supposed to be run as a business. They are also supposed to be run as an instrument of British national policy and Commonwealth cohesion. But they have been run largely to keep alive the British aircraft industry. Whipsawed between three different concepts of direct results, they have done poorly in respect of all three.

Direct results always come first. In the care and feeding of an organization, they play the role calories play in the nutrition of the human body. But any organization also needs a commitment to values and their constant reaffirmation, as a human body needs vitamins and minerals. There has to be something 'this organization stands for', or else it degenerates into disorganization, confusion, and paralysis. In a business, the value commitment may be to technical leadership or (as in Sears Roebuck) to finding the right goods and services for the American family and to procuring them at the lowest price and the best quality.

Value commitments, like results, are not unambiguous.

> The U.S. Department of Agriculture has for many years been torn between two fundamentally incompatible value commitments – one to agricultural productivity and one to the 'family farm' as the 'backbone of the nation'. The former has been pushing the country toward industrial agriculture, highly mechanical, highly industrialized, and essentially a large-scale commercial business. The latter has called for nostalgia supporting a non-producing rural proletariat. But because farm policy – at least until very recently – has wavered between two different value commitments, all it has really succeeded in doing has been to spend prodigious amounts of money.

Organization is, to a large extent, a means of overcoming the limitations mortality sets to what any one man can contribute. An organization that is not capable of perpetuating itself has failed. An organization therefore has to provide today the men who can run it tomorrow. It has to renew its human capital. It should steadily upgrade its human resources. The next generation should take for granted what the hard work and dedication of this generation has accomplished. They should then, standing on the shoulders of their predecessors, establish a new 'high' as the baseline for the generation after them.

An organization which just perpetuates today's level of vision, excellence, and accomplishment has lost the capacity to adapt. And since the one and only thing certain in human affairs is change, it will not be capable of survival in a changed tomorrow.

An executive's focus on contribution by itself is a powerful force in developing people. People adjust to the level of the demands made on them. The executive who sets his sights on contribution, raises the sights and standards of everyone with whom he works.

A new hospital administrator, holding his first staff meeting, thought that a rather difficult matter had been settled to everyone's satisfaction, when one of the participants suddenly asked: 'Would this have satisfied Nurse Bryan?' At once the argument started all over and did not subside until a new and much more ambitious solution to the problem had been hammered out.

Nurse Bryan, the administrator learned, had been a long-serving nurse at the hospital. She was not particularly distinguished, had not, in fact, ever been a supervisor. But whenever a decision on patient care came up on her floor, Nurse Bryan would ask, 'are we doing the best we can do to help this patient?' Patients on Nurse Bryan's floor did better and recovered faster. Gradually over the years, the whole hospital had learned to adopt what came to be known as 'Nurse Bryan's rule', had learned, in other words, to ask: 'Are we really making the best contribution to the purpose of this hospital?'

Though Nurse Bryan herself had retired almost ten years earlier, the standards she had set still made demands on people who in terms of training and position were her superiors.

Commitment to contribution is commitment to responsible effectiveness. Without it, a man short-changes himself, deprives his organization, and cheats the people he works with.

The most common cause of executive failure is inability or unwillingness to change with the demands of a new position. The executive who keeps on doing what he has done successfully before he moved is almost bound to fail. Not only do the results change to which his contribution ought to direct itself. The relative importance between the three dimensions of performance changes. The executive who fails to understand this will suddenly do the wrong things the wrong way – even though he does exactly what in his old job had been the right things done the right way. This was the main reason for the failure of so many able men as executives in World War II Washington. That Washington was 'political' or that men who had always been on their own suddenly found themselves 'cogs in a big machine' were at most contributing factors. Plenty of men proved themselves highly effective Washington executives even though they had no political sense or had never worked in anything bigger than a two-man law practice. Robert E. Sherwood, a most effective administrator in the large Office of War Information (and the author of one of the most perceptive books on effectiveness in power)* had been a playwright whose earlier 'organization' had consisted of his own desk and typewriter.

The men who succeeded in wartime Washington focused on contribution. As a result, they changed both what they did and the relative weight they gave to each of the value dimensions in their work. The failures worked much harder in a good many cases. But they did not challenge themselves, and they failed to see the need for re-directing their efforts.

An outstanding example of success was the man who, already sixty, became chief executive officer of a large nation-wide chain of retail stores. This man had been in the second spot in the company for twenty years or more. He served contentedly under an outgoing and aggressive chief executive officer who was actually several years younger. He never expected to be president himself. But his boss died suddenly while still in his fifties, and the faithful lieutenant had to take over.

The new head had come up as a financial man and was at home with figures – the costing system, purchasing and inventory, the financing of new stores, traffic studies, and so on. People were by and large a shadowy abstraction to him. But when he suddenly found himself president, he asked himself: 'What can I and no one else do which, if done really well, would make a real difference to this company?' The one truly significant contribution, he concluded, would be the development of tomorrow's managers. The company had prided itself for many years on its executive development policies. 'But,' the new chief executive argued, 'a policy does nothing by itself. My contribution is to make sure that this actually gets done.'

From then on for the rest of his tenure, he walked through the

* *Roosevelt and Hopkins* (New York, Harper, 1948).

personnel department three times a week on his way back from lunch and picked up at random eight or ten file folders of young men in the supervisory group. Back in his office, he opened the first folder, scanned it rapidly, and put through a telephone call to the man's superior. 'Mr Robertson, this is the president in New York. You have on your staff a young man, Joe Jones. Didn't you recommend six months ago that he be put in a job where he could acquire some merchandising experience? You did. Why haven't you done anything about it?' And down would go the receiver.

The next folder opened, he would call another manager in another city: 'Mr Smith, this is the president in New York. I understand that you recommended a young man on your staff, Dick Roe, for a job in which he can learn something about store accounting. I just noticed that you have followed through with this recommendation, and I want to tell you how pleased I am to see you working at the development of our young people.'

This man was in the president's chair only a few years before he himself retired. But today, ten or fifteen years later, executives who never met him attribute to him, and with considerable justice, the tremendous growth and success of the company since his time. That he asked himself, 'What can I contribute?' also seems to explain in large part the extraordinary effectiveness of Mr Robert McNamara as U.S. Secretary of Defence – a position for which he was completely unprepared when President Kennedy in the autumn of 1960 plucked him out of the Ford Motor Company and put him into the toughest cabinet job.

McNamara who at Ford had been the perfect 'inside' man, was for instance, totally innocent of politics and tried to leave congressional liaison to subordinates. But after a few weeks, he realized that the Secretary of Defence depends on congressional understanding and support. As a result, he forced himself to do what for so publicity-shy and non-political a man must have been both difficult and distasteful: to cultivate Congress, to get to know the influential men on the congressional committees, and to acquire a mastery of the strange art of congressional in-fighting.

He has perhaps not been completely successful in his dealings with Congress; but he has done better than any earlier secretary.

The McNamara story shows that the higher the position of an executive, the larger will the outside loom in his contribution. No one else in the organization can as a rule move freely on the outside.

Perhaps the greatest shortcoming of the present generation of university presidents in the U.S. is their inside-focus on administration, on money-raising, and so on. Yet no other administrator in the large university is free to establish contact with the students, who are the university's customers; alienation of the students from the administration is certainly a major factor in the student unhappiness and unrest that underlay, for instance, the Berkeley riots at the University of California in 1965.

II. How to Make the Specialist Effective

For the knowledge worker to focus on contribution is particularly important. This alone can enable him to contribute at all.

Knowledge workers do not produce a 'thing'. They produce ideas, information, concepts.

The knowledge worker, moreover, is usually a specialist. In fact, he can, as a rule, be effective only if he has learned to do one thing very well, that is, if he has specialized. By itself, however, a speciality is a fragment and sterile. Its output has to be put together with the output of other specialists before it can produce results.

The task is not to breed generalists. It is to enable the specialist to make himself and his speciality effective. This means that he must think through who is to use his output and what the user needs to know and to understand to be able to make productive the fragment the specialist produces.

It is popular today to believe that our society is divided into 'scientists' and 'laymen'. It is then easy to demand that the layman learn a little bit of the scientist's knowledge, his terminology, his tools, and so on. But if society was ever divided that way, it was a hundred years ago. Today almost everybody in modern organization is an expert with a high degree of specialized knowledge, each with its own tools, its own concerns, and its own jargon. And the sciences, in turn, have all become splintered to the point where one kind of physicist finds it difficult to comprehend what another kind of physicist is concerned with.

The cost accountant is as much a 'scientist' as the biochemist, in the sense that he has his own special area of knowledge with its own assumptions, its own concerns, and its own language. And so is the market researcher and the computer logician, the budget officer of the government agency, and the psychiatric case worker in the hospital. Each of these has to be understood by others before he can be effective.

The man of knowledge has always been expected to take responsibility for being understood. It is barbarian arrogance to assume that the layman can or should make the effort to understand him and that it is enough if the man of knowledge talks to a handful of fellow experts who are his peers. Even in the university or in the research laboratory, this attitude – alas, only too common today – condemns the expert to uselessness and converts his knowledge from learning into pedantry. If a man wants to be an executive, that is, if he wants to be considered responsible for his contribution, he has to concern himself with the usability of his 'product' that is, his knowledge.

Effective executives know this. For they are almost imperceptibly led by their upward orientation into finding out what the other fellow needs, what the other fellow sees, and what the other fellow understands. Effective executives, find themselves asking other people in the organization, their superiors, their subordinates, but above all, their colleagues in other areas: 'What contribution from me do you require to make *your* contribution to the organization? When do you need this, and how do you need it, and in what form?'

If the cost accountant mentioned in Chapter 2 had asked these questions, he would soon have found out which of his assumptions – obvious to him – were totally unfamiliar to the managers who had to use his figures. He would soon have found out which of the figures that to him were important, were irrelevant to the operating people, and which figures, barely seen by him and rarely reported, were the ones they really needed every day.

The biochemist who asks this question in a pharmaceutical company will soon find out that the clinicians can use the findings of the biochemist only if presented in their language rather than in biochemical terms. The clinicians, however, in making the decision whether to put a new compound into clinical testing or not decide whether the biochemist's research product will even have a chance to become a new drug.

The scientist in government who focuses on contribution soon realizes that he must explain to the policy-maker where a scientific development *might* lead to; he must do something forbidden to scientists as a rule, that is, speculate about the outcome of a line of scientific inquiry.

The only meaningful definition of a 'generalist' is a specialist who can relate his own small area to the universe of knowledge. Maybe a few people have knowledge in more than a few small areas. But that does not make them generalists. It makes them specialists in several areas. And one can be just as bigoted in three areas as in one. The man, however, who takes responsibility for his contribution will thereby relate his narrow area to a genuine whole. He may never be able to integrate a number of knowledge areas into one. But he very soon realizes that he has to learn enough of the needs, the directions, the limitations, and the perceptions of others to enable them to use his own work.

Even if this does not make him appreciate the richness and the excitement of diversity, it will give him immunity against the arrogance of the learned, that degenerative disease which destroys knowledge and deprives it of beauty and effectiveness.

III. The Right Human Relations

Executives in an organization do not have good human relations because they have a 'talent for people'. They have good human relations because they focus on contribution in their own work and in their relationships with others. As a result, their relationships are productive – and this is the only valid definition of 'good' human relations. Warm feelings and pleasant words are meaningless, are indeed a false front for wretched attitudes if there is no achievement in what is, after all, a work-focused and task-focused relationship. On the other hand, an occasional rough word will not disturb a relationship that produces results and accomplishments for all concerned.

If I were asked to name the men who, in my own experience, had the best human relations, I would name three: General George C. Marshall, Chief of Staff of the U.S. Army in World War II: Alfred P. Sloan, Jr., the head of General Motors from the early 1920s into the mid-1950s; and one of Sloan's senior associates, Nicholas Dreystadt, the man who built Cadillac into the successful luxury car in the midst of the depression (and might well have been chief executive of General Motors sometime in the 1950s but for his early death right after World War II).

These men were as different as men can be: Marshall, the professional soldier, sparse, austere, dedicated but with great, shy charm; Sloan, the administrator, reserved, polite and very distant; and Dreystadt, warm, bubbling and, superficially, a typical German craftsman of the 'Old Heidelberg' tradition. Every one of them inspired deep devotion, indeed, true affection in all who worked for them. All three, in their different ways, built their relationship to people – their superiors, their colleagues, and their subordinates – around contribution. All three men, of necessity, worked closely with people and thought a good deal about people. All three had to make crucial 'people' decisions. But not one of the three worried about 'human relations'. They took them for granted.

The focus on contribution, by itself supplies the four basic requirements of effective human relations:

- communications;
- teamwork;
- self-development; and,
- development of others.

1. Communications have been in the centre of managerial attention these last twenty years or more. In business, in public administration, in armed services, in hospitals, in other words in all the major institutions of modern society, there has been great concern with communications.

Results to date have been meagre. Communications are by and large just as poor today as they were twenty or thirty years ago when we first became aware of the need for, and lack of, adequate communications in the modern organization.

But we are beginning to understand why this massive communications effort cannot produce results.

We have been working at communications *downward* from management to the employees, from the superior to the subordinate. But communications are practically impossible if they are based on the downward relationship. This much we have learned from our work in perception and communications theory. The harder the superior tries to say something to his subordinate, the more likely is it that the subordinate will mis-hear. He will hear what he expects to hear rather than what is being said.

But executives who take responsibility for contribution in their own work will as a rule demand that their subordinates take responsibility too. They will tend to ask their men: 'What are the contributions for which this organization and I, your superior, should hold you accountable? What should we expect of you? What is the best utilization of your knowledge and your ability?' And then communication becomes possible, becomes indeed easy.

Once the subordinate has thought through what contribution should be expected of him, the superior has, of course, both the right and the responsibility to judge the validity of the proposed contributions.

> According to all our experience, the objectives set for themselves by subordinates are almost never what the superior thought they should be. The subordinates or juniors, in other words, do see reality quite differently. And the more capable they are, the more willing to take responsibility, the more will their perception of reality and of its objective opportunities and needs differ from the view of their superior or of the organization. But any discrepancy between their conclusions and what their superior expected will stand out strongly.

Who is right in such a difference is not as a rule important. For effective communication in meaningful terms has already been established.

2. The focus on contribution leads to communications sideways and thereby makes teamwork possible.

The question 'Who has to use my output for it to become effective?' immediately shows up the importance of people who are not in line of authority, either upward or downward, from and to the individual executive. It underlines what is the reality of a knowledge organization: the effective work is actually done in and by teams of people of diverse knowledges and skills; these people have to work together voluntarily and according to the logic of the situation and the demands of the task, rather than according to a formal jurisdictional structure.

In the hospital, for instance – perhaps the most complex of

the modern knowledge organizations – nurses, dieticians, physical therapists, medical and X-ray technicians, pharmacologists, pathologists, and a host of other health-service professionals, have to work on and with the same patient, with a minimum of conscious command or control by anyone. And yet, they have to work together for a common end and in line with a general plan of action: the doctor's prescription for treatment. In terms of organizational structure, each of these health-service professionals reports to his own chief. Each operates in terms of his own highly specialized field of knowledge, that is, as a 'professional'. But each has to keep all the others informed according to the specific situation, the condition, and the need of an individual patient. Otherwise, their efforts are more likely to do harm than good.

In a hospital in which the focus on contribution has become ingrained habit, there is almost no difficulty in achieving such teamwork. In other hospitals this sideways communication, this spontaneous self-organization into the right task-focused teams does not occur despite frantic efforts to obtain communications and coordination through all kinds of committees, staff conferences, bulletins, sermons, and the like.

The typical institution of today has an organization problem for which traditional concepts and theories are totally inadequate. Knowledge workers must be professionals in their attitude toward their own field of knowledge. They must consider themselves responsible for their own competence and for the standards of their work. In terms of formal organization, they will see themselves as 'belonging' to a functional speciality – whether this is biochemistry or, as in the hospitals, nursing, for example. In terms of their personnel management – their training, their records, but also their appraisal and promotion – they will belong to a knowledge-oriented functional speciality. But in their work they increasingly have to act as responsible members of a team with people from entirely different knowledge areas, organized around the specific task on hand.

Focus on upward contribution will not, by itself, provide the organizational solution. It will, however, contribute understanding of the task and communications to make imperfect organization perform.

Communications within the knowledge work-force is becoming critical as a result of the computer revolution in information. Throughout the ages the problem has always been how to get 'communication' out of 'information'. Because information had to be handled and transmitted by people, it was always distorted by communications, that is, by opinion, impression, comment, judgment, bias, and so on. Now, suddenly, we are in a situation in which information is largely impersonal and, therefore, without any communications content. It is pure information.

But now we have the problem of establishing the necessary minimum of communications so that we understand each other, and can know each other's needs, goals, perceptions, and ways of doing things. Information does not supply this. Only direct contact, whether by voice or by written word, can communicate.

The more we automate information-handling, the more we will have to create opportunities for effective communication.

3. Individual self-development in large measure depends on the focus on contribution.

The man who asks of himself: 'What is the most important contribution I can make to the performance of this organization?' asks, in effect, 'what self-development do I need? What knowledge and skill do I have to acquire to make the contribution I should be making? What strength do I have to put to work? What standards do I have to set myself?'

4. The executive who focuses on contribution also stimulates others to develop themselves whether they are subordinates, colleagues, or superiors. He sets standards which are not personal but grounded in the requirements of the task. At the same time, they are demands for excellence. For they are demands for high aspiration, for ambitious goals, and for work of great impact.

We know very little about self-development. But we do know one thing: people in general, and knowledge workers in particular, grow according to the demands they make on themselves. They grow according to what they consider to be achievement and attainment. If they demand little of themselves, they will remain stunted. If they demand a good deal of themselves, they will grow to giant stature – without any more effort than is expended by the nonachievers.

IV. The Effective Meeting

The meeting, the report or the presentation are the typical work situations of the executive. They are his specific, everyday tools. They also make great demands on his time – even if he succeeds in analysing his time and in controlling whatever can be controlled.

Effective executives know what they expect to get out of a meeting, a report, or a presentation and what the purpose of the occasion is or should be. They ask themselves: 'Why are we having this meeting: do we want a decision, do we want to inform, or do we want to make clear to ourselves what we should be doing?' They will insist that the purpose be thought through and spelled out before a meeting is called, a report asked for, or a presentation organized. They insist that the meeting serve the contribution to which they have committed themselves.

> The effective man always states at the outset of a meeting the specific purpose and contribution it is to achieve. He makes sure that the meeting addresses itself to this purpose. He does not allow a meeting called to inform, to degenerate into a 'bull session' in which everyone has bright ideas. But a meeting called by him to stimulate thinking and ideas also does not become simply a presentation on the part of one of the members, but is run to challenge and stimulate everybody in the room. He always, at the end of his meetings, goes back to the opening statement and relates the final conclusions to the original intent.

There are other rules for making a meeting productive (for instance the obvious but usually disregarded rule that one can either direct a meeting and listen for the important things being said, or one can take part and talk. One cannot do both). But the cardinal rule is to focus it from the start on contribution.

The focus on contribution counteracts one of the basic problems of the executive: the confusion and chaos of events and their failure to indicate by themselves which is meaningful and which is merely 'noise'. The focus on contribution imposes an organizing principle. It imposes relevance on events.

Focusing on contribution turns one of the inherent weaknesses of the executive's situation – his dependence on other people, his being within organization – into a source of strength. It creates a team.

Finally, focusing on contribution fights the temptation to stay within the organization. It leads the executive – especially the top-level man – to lift his eyes from the inside of efforts, work, and relationships, to the outside, that is, to the results of the organization. It makes him try hard to have direct contact with the outside – whether markets and customers, patients in a community, or the various 'publics' which are the outside of a government agency.

To focus on contribution is to focus on effectiveness.

4

Making Strength Productive

The effective executive makes strength productive. He knows that one cannot build on weakness. To achieve results, one has to use all the available strengths – the strengths of associates, the strengths of the superior, and one's own strengths. These strengths are the true opportunities. To make strength productive is the unique purpose of organization. It cannot, of course, overcome the weaknesses with which each of us is abundantly endowed. But it can make them irrelevant. Its task is to use the strength of each man as a building block for joint performance.

I. Staffing From Strength

The area in which the executive first encounters the challenge of strength is in staffing. The effective executive fills positions and promotes on the basis of what a man can do. He does not make staffing decisions to minimize weaknesses but to maximize strength.

President Lincoln, when told that General Grant, his new commander-in-chief, was fond of the bottle said: 'If I knew his brand, I'd send a barrel or so of it to some other generals.' After a childhood on the Kentucky and Illinois frontier, Lincoln assuredly knew all about the bottle and its dangers. But of all the Union generals, Grant alone had proven consistently capable of planning and leading winning campaigns. Grant's appointment was the turning point of the Civil War. It was an effective appointment because Lincoln chose his general for his tested ability to win battles and not for his sobriety, that is, for the absence of a weakness.

Lincoln learned this the hard way however. Before he chose Grant, he had appointed in succession three or four generals whose main qualifications were their lack of major weaknesses. As a result, the North, despite its tremendous superiority in men and material, had not made any headway for three long years from 1861 to 1864. In sharp contrast, Lee, in command of the Confederate forces, had staffed from strength. Every one of Lee's generals, from Stonewall Jackson on, was a man of obvious and monumental weaknesses. But these failings Lee considered – rightly – to be irrelevant. Each of them had, however, one area of real strength – and it was this strength, and only this strength, that Lee utilized and made effective. As a result, the 'well-rounded' men Lincoln had appointed were beaten time and again by Lee's 'single-purpose tools', the men of narrow but very great strength.

Whoever tries to place a man or staff an organization to avoid weakness will end up at best with mediocrity. The idea that there are 'well-rounded' people, people who have only strengths and no weaknesses (whether the term used is the 'whole man', the 'mature personality', the 'well-adjusted personality', or the 'generalist') is a prescription for mediocrity if not for incompetence. Strong people always have strong weaknesses too. Where there are peaks, there are valleys. And no one is strong in many areas. Measured against the universe of human knowledge, experience, and abilities, even the greatest genius would have to be rated a total failure. There is no such thing as a 'good man'. Good for what? is the question.

The executive who is concerned with what a man cannot do rather than with what he can do, and who therefore tries to avoid weakness rather than make strength effective is a weak man himself. He probably sees strength in others as a threat to himself. But no executive has ever suffered because his subordinates were strong and effective. There is no prouder boast, but also no better prescription, for executive effectiveness than the words Andrew Carnegie, the father of the U.S. steel industry, chose for his own tombstone: 'Here lies a man who knew how to bring into his service men better than he was himself.' But of course every one of these men was 'better' because Carnegie looked for his strength and put it to work. Each of these steel executives was a 'better man' in one specific area and for one specific job. Carnegie, however, was the effective executive among them.

Another story about General Robert E. Lee illustrates the meaning of making strength productive. One of his generals, the story goes, had disregarded orders and had thereby completely upset Lee's plans – and not for the first time either. Lee, who normally controlled his temper, blew up in a towering rage. When he had simmered down one of his aides asked respectfully, 'Why don't you relieve him of his command?' Lee, it is said, turned around in complete amazement, looked at the aide, and said, 'What an absurd question – he performs.'

Effective executives know that their subordinates are paid to perform and not to please their superiors. They know that it does not matter how many tantrums a primadonna throws as long as she brings in the customers. The opera manager is paid after all for putting up with the primadonna's tantrums, if that is her way to achieve excellence in performance. It does not matter whether a first-rate teacher or a brilliant scholar is pleasant to the dean or amiable in the faculty meeting. The dean is paid for enabling the first-rate teacher or the first-rate scholar to do his work effectively – and if this involves unpleasantness in the administrative routine, it is still cheap at the price.

Effective executives never ask 'How does he get along with me?' Their question is: 'What does he contribute?' Their question is never: 'What can a man not do?' Their question is always: 'What can he do uncommonly well?' In staffing they look for excellence in one major area, and not for performance that gets by all around.

To look for one area of strength and to attempt to put it to work is dictated by the nature of man. In fact, all the talk of 'the whole man' or the 'mature personality' hides a profound contempt for man's most specific gift: his ability to put all his resources behind one activity, one field of endeavour, one area of accomplishment. It is, in other words, contempt for excellence. Human excellence can only be achieved in one area, or at the most in very few.

People with many interests do exist – and this is usually what we mean when we talk of a 'universal genius'. People with outstanding accomplishments in many areas are unknown. Even Leonardo performed only in the area of design despite his manifold interests; if Goethe's poetry had been lost and all that were known of his work were his dabblings in optics and philosophy, he would not even rate a footnote in the most learned encyclopaedia. What is true for the giants holds doubly for the rest of us. Unless, therefore, an executive looks for strength and works at making strength productive, he will only get the impact of what a man cannot do, of his lacks, his weaknesses, his impediments to performance and effectiveness. To staff from what there is not and to focus on weakness is wasteful – a misuse, if not abuse, of the human resource.

To focus on strength is to make demands for performance. The man who does not first ask, 'What can a man do?' is bound to accept far less than the associate can really contribute. He excuses the associate's non-performance in advance. He is destructive but not critical, let alone realistic. The really 'demanding boss' – and one way or another all makers of men are demanding bosses – always starts out with what a man should be able to do well – and then demands that he really do it.

To try to build against weakness frustrates the purpose of organization. Organization is the specific instrument to make human strengths redound to performance while human weakness is neutralized and largely rendered harmless. The very strong neither need nor desire organization. They are much better off working on their own. The rest of us, however, the great majority, do not have so much strength that by itself it would become effective despite our limitations. 'One cannot hire a hand – the whole man always comes with it,' says a proverb of the human relations people. Similarly, one cannot by oneself be only strong; the weaknesses are always with us.

But we can so structure an organization that the weaknesses become a personal blemish outside of, or at least beside, the work and accomplishment. We can so structure as to make the strength relevant.

A good tax accountant in private practice might be greatly hampered by his inability to get along with people. But in an organization such a man can be set up in an office of his own and shielded from direct contact with other people. In an organization one can make his strength effective and his weakness irrelevant. The small businessman who is good at finance but poor at production or marketing is likely to get into trouble. In a somewhat larger business one can easily make productive a man who has true strength in finance alone.

Effective executives are not blind to weakness. The executive who understands that it is his job to enable John Jones to do his tax accounting has no illusions about Jones's ability to get along with people. He would never appoint Jones a manager. But there are others who get along with people. First-rate tax accountants are a good deal rarer. Therefore, what this man – and many others like him – can do is pertinent in an organization. What he cannot do is a limitation and nothing else.

All this is obvious, one might say. Why, then, is it not done all the time? Why are executives rare who make strength productive – especially the strength of their associates? Why did even a Lincoln staff from weakness three times before he picked strength?

The main cause is that the immediate task of the executive is not to place a man; it is to fill a job. The tendency is therefore to start out with the job as being a part of the order of nature. Then one looks for a man to fill the job. It is only too easy to be misled this way into looking for the 'least misfit' – the one man who leaves least to be desired. And this is invariably the mediocrity.

The widely advertised 'cure' for this is to structure jobs to fit the personalities available. But this cure is worse than the disease – except perhaps in a very small and simple organization. Jobs have to be objective, that is, determined by task rather than by personality.

One reason for this is that every change in the definition, structure, and position of a job within an organization sets off a chain reaction of changes throughout the entire institution. Jobs in an organization are interdependent and interlocked. One cannot change everybody's work and responsibility just because one has to replace a single man in a single job. To structure one job to a person is almost certain to result in the end in greater discrepancy between the demands of the job and the available talent. It results in a dozen people being uprooted and pushed around in order to accommodate one.

This is by no means true only of bureaucratic organizations such as a government agency or a large business corporation. Somebody has to teach the introductory course in biochemistry in the university. It had better be a good man. Such a man will be a specialist. Yet the course has to be general and has to include the foundation materials of the discipline, regardless of the interests and inclinations of the teacher. What is to be taught is determined by what the students need, that is, by an objective requirement, which the individual instructor has to accept. When the orchestra conductor has to fill the job of first 'cellist, he will not even consider a poor 'cellist who is a first-rate oboe player even though the oboist might be a greater musician than any of the available 'cellists. The conductor will not rewrite the score to accommodate a man. The opera manager who knows that he is being paid for putting up with the tantrums of the primadonna still expects her to sing 'Tosca' when the playbill announces *Tosca*.

But there is a subtler reason for insistence on impersonal, objective jobs. It is the only way to provide the organization with the human diversity it needs. It is the only way to tolerate – indeed to encourage – differences in temperament and personality in an organization. To tolerate diversity, relationships must be task-focused rather than personality-focused. Achievement must be measured against objective criteria of contribution and performance. This is possible, however, only if jobs are defined and structured impersonally. Otherwise the accent will at once be on 'Who is right?' rather than on 'What is right?' In no time, personnel decisions will be made on 'Do I like this fellow?' or 'Will he be acceptable?' rather than by asking: 'Is he the man most likely to do an outstanding job?'

Structuring jobs to fit personality is almost certain to lead to favouritism and conformity. And no organization can afford either. It needs equity and impersonal fairness in its personnel decisions. Or else it will either lose its good people or destroy their incentive. And it needs diversity. Or else it will lack the ability to change and the ability for dissent which (as Chapter 7 will discuss) the right decision demands.

One implication is that the men who build first-class executive teams are not usually close to their immediate colleagues and subordinates. Picking people for what they can do, rather than on personal likes or dislikes, they seek performance, not conformance. To insure this outcome, they keep a distance between themselves and their close colleagues.

Lincoln, it has often been remarked, only became an effective chief executive after he had changed from close personal relations – e.g. with Stanton, his Secretary of War – to aloofness and distance. Franklin D. Roosevelt had no 'friend' in the cabinet – not even Henry Morgenthau, his Secretary of the Treasury, and a close friend in all non-governmental matters. General Marshall and Alfred P. Sloan were similarly remote. These were all warm men, in need of close human relationships, endowed with the gift of making and keeping friends. They knew, however, that their friendships had to be 'off the job'. They knew that whether they liked a man or approved of him was irrelevant, if not a distraction. And by staying aloof they were able to build teams of great diversity but also of strength.

Of course, there are always exceptions where the job should be fitted to the man. Even Sloan, despite his insistence on impersonal structure, consciously designed the early engineering organization of General Motors around a man, Charles F. Kettering, the great inventor. Roosevelt broke every rule in the book to enable the dying Harry Hopkins to make his unique contribution. But these exceptions should be rare. And they should only be made for a man who has proven exceptional capacity to do the unusual with excellence.

How then do effective executives staff for strength without stumbling into the opposite trap of building jobs to suit personality?

By and large they follow four rules:

1. They do not start out with the assumption that jobs are created by nature or by God. They know that they have been designed by highly fallible men. And they are therefore forever on guard against the 'impossible' job, the job that simply is not for normal human beings.

Such jobs are common. They usually look exceedingly logical on paper. But they cannot be filled. One man of proven performance capacity after the other is tried – and none does well. Six months or a year later, the job has defeated them.

Almost always such a job was first created to accommodate an unusual man and tailored to his idiosyncrasies. It usually calls for a mixture of temperaments that is rarely found in one person. Individuals can acquire very divergent kinds of knowledge and highly disparate skills. But they cannot change their temperaments. A job that calls for disparate temperaments becomes an 'un-doable' job, a man-killer.

The rule is simple: Any job that has defeated two or three men in succession, even though each had performed well in his previous assignments, must be assumed unfit for human beings. It must be re-designed.

Every text on marketing concludes, for instance, that sales management belongs together with advertising and promotion and under the same marketing executive. The experience of large, national manufacturers of branded and mass-marketed consumer goods has been, however, that this overall marketing job is impossible. Such a business needs both high effectiveness in field-selling, that is in moving goods, and high effectiveness in advertising and promotion, that is in moving people. These appeal to different personalities which rarely can be found in one man.

The presidency of a large university in the United States is also such an impossible job. At least our experience has been that only a small minority of the appointments to this position work out – even though the men chosen have almost always a long history of substantial achievement in earlier assignments.

Another example is probably the international vice-president of today's large multi-national business. As soon as production and sales outside the parent company's territory become significant – as soon as they exceed one fifth of the total or so – putting everything that is 'not parent company' in one organizational component creates an impossible, a man-killing, job. The work either has to be reorganized by world-wide product-groups (as Philips in Holland has done, for instance) or according to common social and economic characteristics of major markets. For instance, it might be split into three jobs, one managing the business in industrialized countries (Western Europe, Japan), one the business in the developing countries (most of Latin America, Australia, India, the Near East), one the business in remaining underdeveloped ones. Several major chemical companies are going this route.

The ambassador of a major power today is in a similar predicament. His embassy has become so huge, unwieldy, and diffuse in its activities that a man who can administer it has no time for, and almost certainly no interest in, his first job: getting to know the country of his assignment, its government, its policies, its people, and to get known and trusted by them. And despite Mr McNamara's lion-taming act at the Pentagon, I am not yet convinced that the job of Secretary of Defence of the United States is really possible (though I admit I cannot conceive of an alternative).

The effective executive therefore first makes sure that the job is well-designed. And if experience tells him otherwise, he does not hunt for genius to do the impossible. He re-designs the job. He knows that the test of organization is not genius. It is its capacity to make common people achieve uncommon performance.

2. The second rule for staffing from strength is to make each job demanding and big. It should have challenge to bring out whatever strength a man may have. It should have scope so that any strength that is relevant to the task can produce significant results.

This, however, is not the policy of most large organizations. They tend to make the job small – which would make sense only if people were designed and machined for specific performance at a given moment. Yet not only do we have to fill jobs with people as they come. The demands of any job above the simplest are also bound to change, and often abruptly. The 'perfect fit' then rapidly becomes the misfit. Only if the job is big and demanding to begin with, will it enable a man to rise to the new demands of a changed situation.

This rule applies in particular to the job of the beginning knowledge worker. Whatever his strength it should have a chance to find full play. In his first job the standards are set by which a knowledge worker will guide himself the rest of his career and by which he will measure himself and his contribution. Till he enters the first adult job, the knowledge worker never has had a chance to perform. All one can do in school is to show promise. Performance is possible only in real work, whether in a research lab, in a teaching job, in a business or in a government agency. Both for the beginner in knowledge work and for the rest of the organization, his colleagues and his superiors, the most important thing to find out is what he really can do.

It is equally important for him to find out as early as possible whether he is indeed in the right place, or even in the right kind of work. There are fairly reliable tests for the aptitudes and skills needed in manual work. One can test in advance whether a man is likely to do well as a carpenter or as a machinist. There is no such test appropriate to knowledge work. What is needed in knowledge work is not this or that particular skill, but a configuration; and this will be revealed only by the test of performance.

A carpenter's or a machinist's job is defined by the craft and varies little from one shop to another. But for the ability of a knowledge worker to contribute in an organization, the values and the goals of the organization are at least as important as his own professional knowledge and skills. A young man who has the right strength for one organization may be a total misfit in another, which from the outside looks just the same. The first job should, therefore, enable him to test both himself and the organization.

This not only holds for different kinds of organization, such as government agencies, universities or businesses. It is equally true between organizations of the same kind. I have yet to see two large businesses which have the same values and stress the same contributions. That a man who was happy and productive as a member of the faculty of one university may find himself lost, unhappy, and frustrated when he moves to another one every academic administrator has learned. And no matter how much the Civil Service Commission tries to make all government departments observe the same rules and use the same yardsticks, government agencies, once they have been in existence for a few years, have a distinct personality. Each requires a different behaviour from its staff members, especially from those in the professional grades, to be effective and to make a contribution.

It is easy to move while young – at least in the Western countries where mobility is accepted. Once one has been in an organization for ten years or more, however, it becomes increasingly difficult, especially for those who have not been too effective. The young knowledge worker should, therefore, ask himself early: 'Am I in the right work and in the right place for my strengths to tell?'

But he cannot ask this question, let alone answer it, if the beginning job is too small, too easy, and designed to offset his lack of experience rather than to bring out what he can do.

Every survey of young knowledge workers – physicians in the Army Medical Corps, chemists in the research lab, accountants or engineers in the plant, nurses in the hospital – produces the same results. The ones who are enthusiastic and who, in turn, have results to show for their work, are the ones whose abilities are being challenged and used. Those that are deeply frustrated all say, in one way or another: 'My abilities are not being put to use.'

The young knowledge worker whose job is too small to challenge and test his abilities either leaves or declines rapidly into premature middle age, soured, cynical, unproductive. Executives everywhere complain that many young men with fire in their bellies turn so soon into burnt-out sticks. They have only themselves to blame: they quenched the fire by making the young man's job too small.

3. Effective executives know that they have to start with what a man can do rather than with what a job requires. This, however, means that they do their thinking about people long before the decision on filling a job has to be made, and independently of it.

This is the reason for the wide adoption of appraisal procedures today in which people, especially those in knowledge work, are regularly judged. The purpose is to arrive at an appraisal of a man *before* one has to decide whether he is the right person to fill a bigger position.

However, while almost every large organization has an appraisal procedure, few of them actually use it. Again and again the same executives who say that of course they appraise every one of their subordinates at least once a year, report that, to the best of their knowledge, they themselves have never been appraised by their own superiors. Again and again the appraisal forms remain in the files, and nobody looks at them when a personnel decision has to be made. Everybody dismisses them as so much useless paper. Above all, almost without exception, the 'appraisal interview' in which the superior is to sit down with the subordinate and discuss the findings never takes place. Yet the appraisal interview is the crux of the whole system. One clue to what is wrong was contained in an advertisement of a new book on management which talked of the appraisal interview as 'the most distasteful job' of the superior.

Appraisals, as they are now being used in the great majority of organizations, were designed originally by the clinical and abnormal psychologists for their own purposes. The clinician is a therapist trained to heal the sick. He is legitimately concerned with what is wrong, rather than with what is right with the patient. He assumes as a matter of course that nobody comes to him unless he is in trouble. The clinical psychologist or the abnormal psychologist, therefore, very properly looks upon appraisals as a process of diagnosing the weaknesses of a man.

I became aware of this in my first exposure to Japanese management. Running a seminar on executive development, I found to my surprise that none of the Japanese participants – all top men in large organizations – used appraisals. When I asked why not, one of them said: 'Your appraisals are concerned only with bringing out a man's faults and weaknesses. Since we can neither fire a man nor deny him advancement and promotion, this is of no interest to us. On the contrary, the less we know about his weaknesses, the better. What we do need to know are the strengths of a man and what he can do. Your appraisals are not even interested in this.' Western psychologists – especially those that design appraisals – might well disagree. But this is how every executive, whether Japanese, American, or German sees the traditional appraisal.

Altogether the West might well ponder the lessons of the Japanese achievement. As everyone has heard, there is 'lifetime employment' in Japan. Once a man is on the payroll, he will advance in his category – as a worker, a white-collar employee, or a professional and executive employee – according to his age and length of service, with his salary doubling about once every fifteen years. He cannot leave, neither can he be fired. Only at the top and after age 45 is there differentiation, with a very small group selected by ability and merit into the senior executive positions. How can such a system be squared with the tremendous capacity for results and achievement Japan has shown? The answer is that their system forces the Japanese to play down weaknesses. Precisely because they cannot move people, Japanese executives always look for the man in the group who can do the job. They always look for strength.

I do not recommend the Japanese system. It is far from ideal. A very small number of people who have proven their capacity to perform, do, in effect, everything of any importance whatever. The rest are carried by the organization. But if we in the West expect to get the benefit of the much greater mobility that both individual and organization enjoy in our tradition, we had better adopt the Japanese custom of looking for strength and using strength.

For a superior to focus on weakness, as our appraisals require him to do, destroys the integrity of his relationship with his subordinates. The many executives who in effect sabotage the appraisals their policy manuals impose on them follow sound instinct. It is also perfectly understandable that they consider an appraisal interview that focuses on a search for faults, defects, and weaknesses distasteful. To discuss a man's defects when he comes in as a patient seeking help is the responsibility of the healer. But, as has been known since Hippocrates, this presupposes a professional and privileged relationship between healer and patient which is incompatible with the authority-relationship between superior and subordinate. It is a relationship that makes continued working together almost impossible. That so few executives use the official appraisal is thus hardly surprising. It is the wrong tool, in the wrong situation, for the wrong purpose.

Appraisal – and the philosophy behind it – are also far too much concerned with 'potential'. But experienced people have learned that one cannot appraise potential for any length of time ahead or for anything very different from what a man is already doing. 'Potential' is simply another word for 'promise'. And even if the promise is there, it may well go unfulfilled, while people who have not shown such promise (if only because they may not have had the opportunity) actually produce the performance.

All one can measure is performance. And all one should measure is performance. This is another reason for making jobs big and challenging. It is also a reason for thinking through the contribution a man should make to the results and the performance of his organization. For one can measure the performance of a man only against specific performance expectations.

Still one needs some form of appraisal procedure – or else one makes the personnel evaluation at the wrong time, that is when a job has to be filled. Effective executives, therefore, usually work out their own radically different form. It starts out with a statement of the major contributions expected from a man in his past and present positions and a record of his performance against these goals. Then it asks four questions:

A. 'What has he (or she) done well?'
B. 'What, therefore, is he likely to be able to do well?'
C. 'What does he have to learn or to acquire to be able to get the full benefit from his strength?'
D. 'If I had a son or daughter, would I be willing to have him or her work under this person?'
(a) 'If yes, why?'
(b) 'If no, why?'

This appraisal actually takes a much more critical look at a man than the usual procedure does. But it focuses on strengths. It begins with what a man can do. Weaknesses are seen as limitations to the full use of his strengths and to his own achievement, effectiveness, and accomplishment.

The last question (b) is the only one which is not primarily concerned with strengths. Subordinates, especially bright, young, and ambitious ones, tend to mould themselves after a forceful boss. There is, therefore, nothing more corrupting and more destructive in an organization than a forceful but basically corrupt executive. Such a man might well operate effectively on his own; even within an organization, he might be tolerable if denied all power over others. But in a position of power within an organization, he destroys. Here, therefore, is the one area in which weakness in itself is of importance and relevance.

By themselves character and integrity do not accomplish anything. But their absence faults everything else. Here, therefore, is the one area where weakness is a disqualification in itself rather than a limitation in performance capacity and strength.

4. The effective executive knows that to get strength one has to put up with weaknesses.

There have been few great commanders in history who were not self-centred, conceited, and full of admiration for what they saw in the mirror. (The reverse does not, of course, hold: there have been plenty of generals who were convinced of their own greatness, but who have not gone down in history as great commanders.) Similarly, the politician who does not with every fibre in his body want to be President or Prime Minister is not likely to be remembered as a statesman. He will at best be a useful – perhaps a highly useful – journeyman. To be more requires a man who is conceited enough to believe that the world – or at least the nation – really needs him and depends on his getting into power. (Again the reverse does not hold true.) If the need is for the ability to command in a perilous situation, one has to accept a Disraeli or a Franklin D. Roosevelt and not worry too much about their lack of humility. There are indeed no great men to their valets. But the laugh is on the valet. He sees, inevitably, all the traits that are not relevant, all the traits that have nothing to do with the specific task for which a man has been called on the stage of history.

The effective executive will therefore ask: 'Does this man have strength in *one* major area? And is this strength relevant to the task? If he achieves excellence in this one area, will it make a significant difference?'

And if the answer is 'yes' he will go ahead and appoint the man.

Effective executives rarely suffer from the delusion that two mediocrities achieve as much as one good man. They have learned that, as a rule, two mediocrities achieve even less than one mediocrity – they just get in each other's way. They accept that abilities must be specific to produce performance. They never talk of a 'good man' but always about a man who is 'good' for some one task. But in this one task, they search for strength and staff for excellence.

This also implies that they focus on opportunity in their staffing – not on problems.

They are above all intolerant of the argument: 'I can't spare this man; I'd be in trouble without him.' They have learned that there are only three explanations for an 'indispensable man': he is actually incompetent and can only survive if carefully shielded from demands; his strength is misused to bolster a weak superior who cannot stand on his own two feet; or his strength is misused to delay tackling a serious problem if not to conceal its existence.

In every one of these situations, the 'indispensable man' should be moved anyhow – and soon. Otherwise one only destroys whatever strengths he may have.

> The chief executive who was mentioned earlier in Chapter 3 for his unconventional methods of making effective the manager-development policies of a large retail chain, also decided to move automatically anyone whose boss described him as indispensable. 'This either means,' he said, 'that I have a weak superior or a weak subordinate – or both. Whichever of these, the sooner we find out, the better.'

Altogether it must be an unbreakable rule to promote the man who by the test of performance is best qualified for the job to be filled. All arguments to the contrary – 'he is indispensable' . . . 'he won't be acceptable to the people there' . . . 'he is too young' . . . or 'we never put a man in there without field experience' – should be given short shrift. Not only does the job deserve the best man. The man of proven performance has earned the opportunity. Staffing the opportunities instead of the problems not only creates the most effective organization. It also creates enthusiasm and dedication.

Conversely, it is the duty of the executive to remove ruthlessly anyone – and especially any manager – who consistently fails to perform with high distinction. To let such a man stay on corrupts the others. It is grossly unfair to the whole organization. It is grossly unfair to his subordinates who are deprived by their superior's inadequacy of opportunities for achievement and recognition. Above all, it is senseless cruelty to the man himself. He knows that he is inadequate whether he admits it to himself or not. Indeed I have never seen anyone in a job for which he was inadequate who was not slowly being destroyed by the pressure and the strains, and who did not secretly pray for deliverance. That neither the Japanese 'lifetime employment' nor the various civil-service systems of the West consider proven incompetence ground for removal is a serious weakness – and an unnecessary one.

General Marshall during World War II insisted that a general officer be immediately relieved if found less than outstanding. To keep him in command, he reasoned, was incompatible with the responsibility the Army and the nation owed the men under an officer's command. Marshall flatly refused to listen to the argument: 'But we have no replacement.' 'All that matters,' he pointed out, 'is that you know that this man is not equal to the task. Where his replacement comes from is the next question.'

But Marshall also insisted that to relieve a man from command was less a judgment on the man than on the commander who had appointed him. 'The only thing we know is that this spot was the wrong one for the man,' he argued. 'This does not mean that he is not the ideal man for some other job. Appointing him was my mistake, now it's up to me to find what he can do.'

Altogether General Marshall offers a good example of how one makes strength productive. When he first reached a position of influence in the mid-thirties, there was no general officer in the U.S. Army still young enough for active duty. (Marshall himself only beat the deadline by four months. His sixtieth birthday when he would have been too old to take office as Chief of Staff was on 31 December 1939. He was appointed on 1 September, of the same year.) The future generals of World War II were still junior officers with few hopes for promotion when Marshall began to select and train them. Eisenhower was one of the older ones and even he at that time was only a major. Yet by 1942, Marshall had developed the largest and clearly the ablest group of general officers in American history. There were almost no failures in it and not too many second-raters.

This – one of the greatest educational feats in military history – was done by a man who lacked all the normal trappings of 'leadership', such as the personal magnetism or the towering self-confidence of a Montgomery, a de Gaulle, or a MacArthur. What Marshall had were principles. 'What can this man do?' was his constant question. And if a man could do something, his lacks became secondary.

> Marshall, for instance, again and again came to George Patton's rescue and made sure that this ambitious, vain, but powerful wartime commander would not be penalized for the absence of the qualities that make a good staff officer and a successful career soldier in peacetime. Yet Marshall himself personally loathed the dashing *beau sabreur* of Patton's type.

Marshall was only concerned with weaknesses when they limited the full development of a man's strength. These he tried to overcome through work and career opportunities.

> The young Major Eisenhower, for instance, was quite deliberately put by Marshall into war-planning in the mid-1930s to help him acquire the systematic strategic understanding which he apparently lacked. Eisenhower did not himself become a strategist as a result. But he acquired respect for strategy and an understanding of its importance and thereby removed a serious limitation on his great strength as a team-builder and tactical planner.

Marshall always appointed the best qualified man no matter how badly he was needed where he was. 'We owe this move to the job . . . we owe it to the man and we owe it to the troops,' was his reply when someone – usually someone high up – pleaded with him not to pull out an 'indispensable' man.

> He made but one exception: when President Roosevelt pleaded that Marshall was indispensable to him, Marshall stayed in Washington, yielded supreme command in Europe to Eisenhower, and thus gave up his life's dream.

Finally Marshall knew – and everyone can learn it from him –

that every people-decision is a gamble. By basing it on what a man can do, it becomes at least a rational gamble.

A superior has responsibility for the work of others. He also has power over the careers of others. Making strengths productive is therefore much more than an essential of effectiveness. It is a moral imperative, a responsibility of authority and position. To focus on weakness is not only foolish; it is irresponsible. A superior owes it to his organization to make the strength of every one of his subordinates as productive as it can be. But even more does he owe it to the human beings over whom he exercises authority to help them get the most out of whatever strength they may have.

Organization must serve the individual to achieve through his strengths and regardless of his limitations and weaknesses.

This is becoming increasingly important, indeed critical. Only a short generation ago the number of knowledge jobs and the range of knowledge employments were small. To be a civil servant in the German or in the Scandinavian governments, one had to have a law degree. A mathematician need not apply. Conversely a young man wanting to make a living by putting his knowledge to work had only three or four choices of fields and employment. Today there is a bewildering variety of knowledge work and an equally bewildering variety of employment choices for men of knowledge. Around 1900, the only knowledge fields for all practical purposes were still the traditional professions – the law, medicine, teaching, and preaching. There are now literally hundreds of different disciplines. Moreover, practically every knowledge area is being put to productive use in and by organization, especially, of course, by business and government.

On the one hand, therefore, one can today try to find the knowledge area and the kind of work to which one's abilities are best fitted. One need no longer, as one had to do even in the recent past, fit oneself to the available knowledge areas and employments. On the other hand, it is increasingly difficult for a young man to make this choice. He does not have enough information, either about himself, or about the opportunities.

This makes it much more important for the individual that he be directed toward making his strengths productive. It also makes it important for the organization that its executives focus on strengths and work on making strengths productive in their own group and with their own subordinates.

Staffing for strength is thus essential to the executive's own effectiveness and to that of his organization but equally to individual and society in a world of knowledge work.

II. How Do I Manage My Boss?

Above all, the effective executive tries to make fully productive the strength of his own superior.

I have yet to find a manager, whether in business, in government or in any other institution, who did not say: 'I have no great trouble managing my subordinates. But how do I manage my boss?' It is actually remarkably easy – but only effective executives know that. The secret is that effective executives make the strengths of the boss productive.

This should be elementary prudence. Contrary to popular legend, subordinates do not, as a rule, rise to position and prominence over the prostrate bodies of incompetent bosses. If their boss is not promoted, they will tend to be bottled up behind him. And if their boss is relieved for incompetence or failure, the successor is rarely the bright, young man next in line. He usually is brought in from the outside and brings with him his own bright, young men. Conversely, there is nothing quite as conducive to success as a successful and rapidly promoted superior.

But way beyond prudence, making the strength of the boss productive is a key to the subordinate's own effectiveness. It enables him to focus his own contribution in such a way that it finds receptivity upstairs and will be put to use. It enables him to achieve and accomplish the things he himself believes in.

One does not make the strengths of the boss productive by toadying to him. One does it by starting out with what is right and presenting it in a form which is accessible to the superior.

The effective executive accepts that the boss is human (something that intelligent young subordinates often find hard). Because the superior is human, he has his strengths; but he also has limitations. To build on his strength, that is, to enable him to do what he can do, will make him effective – and will make the subordinate effective. To try to build on his weaknesses will be as frustrating and as stultifying as to try to build on the weaknesses of a subordinate. The effective executive, therefore, asks: 'What can my boss do really well?' 'What has he done really well?' 'What does he need to know to use his strength?' 'What does he need to get from me to perform?' He does not worry too much over what the boss cannot do.

Subordinates typically want to 'reform' the boss. The able senior civil servant is inclined to see himself as the tutor to the newly appointed political head of his agency. He tries to get his boss to overcome his limitations. The effective ones ask instead: 'What can the new boss do?' And if the answer is: 'He is good at relationships with Congress, the White House, and the public,' then the civil servant works at making it possible for his minister to use these abilities. For the best administration and the best policy decisions are futile unless there is also political skill in representing them. Once the politician knows that the civil servant supports him, he will soon enough listen to him on policy and on administration.

The effective executive also knows that the boss being human has his own ways of being effective. He looks for these ways. They may be only manners and habits, but they are facts.

It is, I submit, fairly obvious to anyone who has ever looked, that people are either 'readers' or 'listeners', excepting only the very small group who get their information through talking, and by watching with a form of psychic radar the reactions of the people they talk to. (Both President Franklin Roosevelt and President Lyndon Johnson belong in this category, as apparently did Winston Churchill.)

People who are both readers and listeners – trial lawyers have to be both, as a rule – are exceptions. It is, generally a waste of time to talk to a reader. He only listens after he has read. It is equally a waste of time to submit a voluminous report to a listener. He can only grasp what it is all about through the spoken word.

Some people need to have things summed up for them in one page. (President Eisenhower needed this to be able to act.) Others need to be able to follow the thought processes of the man who makes the recommendation and therefore require a big report before anything becomes meaningful to them. Some superiors want to see sixty pages of figures on everything. Some want to be in at the early stages so that they can prepare themselves for the eventual decision. Others do not want even to hear about the matter until it is 'ripe', and so on.

The adaptation needed to think through the strengths of the boss and to try to make them productive always affects the 'how' rather than the 'what'. It concerns the order in which different areas, all of them relevant, are presented, rather than what is important or right. If the superior's strength lies in his political ability in a job in which political ability is truly relevant, then one presents to him first the political aspect of a situation. This enables him to grasp what the issue is all about and to put his strength effectively behind a new policy.

All of us are 'experts' on other people and see them much more clearly than they see themselves. To make the boss effective is therefore usually fairly easy. But it requires focus on his strengths and on what he can do. It requires building on strength to make weaknesses irrelevant. Few things make an executive as effective as building on the strengths of his superior.

III. Making Yourself Effective

Effective executives lead from strength in their own work. They make productive what they can do.

Most executives I know in government, in the hospital, in a business, know all the things they cannot do. They are only too conscious of what the boss won't let them do, of what company policy won't let them do, of what the government won't let them do, and so on. As a result, they waste their time and their strengths complaining about the things they cannot do anything about.

Effective executives are, of course, also concerned with limitations. But it is amazing how many things they find that can be done and are worth while doing. While the others complain about their inability to do anything, the effective executives go ahead and do. As a result, the limitations that weigh so heavily on their brethren often melt away.

> Everyone in the management of one of the major railroads knew that the government would not let the company do anything. But then a new financial vice-president came in who had not yet learned that 'lesson'. Instead he went to Washington, called on the Interstate Commerce Commission, and asked for permission to do a few rather radical things. 'Most of these

things,' the commissioner said, 'are none of our concern to begin with. The others you have to try and test out and then we will be glad to give you the go-ahead.'

The assertion that 'somebody else will not let me do anything' should always be suspected as a cover-up for inertia. But even where the situation does set limitations – and everyone lives and works within rather stringent limitations – there are usually important, meaningful, pertinent things that can be done.

The effective executive looks for them. If he starts out with the question: 'What can I do?' he is almost certain to find that he can actually do much more than he has time and resources for.

Making strengths productive is equally important in respect to one's own abilities and work habits.

It is not very difficult to know *how* we achieve results. By the time one has reached adulthood, one has a pretty good idea as to whether one works better in the morning or at night. One usually knows whether one writes best by making a great many drafts fast, or by working meticulously on every sentence until it is right. One knows whether one speaks well in public from a prepared text, from notes, without any prop, or not at all. One knows whether one works well as a member of a committee or better alone – or whether one is altogether unproductive as a committee member.

Some people work best if they have a detailed outline in front of them, that is, if they have thought through the job before they start it. Others work best with nothing more than a few rough notes. Some work best under pressure. Others work better if they have a good deal of time and can finish the job long before the deadline. Some are 'readers', others, 'listeners'. All this one knows about oneself – just as one knows whether he is right-handed or left-handed.

These, it will be said, are superficial. This is not necessarily correct – a good many of these traits and habits mirror fundamentals of a man's personality such as his perception of the world and of himself in it. But even if superficial, these work habits are a source of effectiveness. And most of them are compatible with any kind of work.

The effective executive knows this and acts accordingly.

Altogether the effective executive tries to be himself; he does not pretend to be someone else. He looks at his own performance and at his own results and tries to discern a pattern. 'What are the things,' he asks 'that I seem to be able to do with relative ease, while they come rather hard to other people?' One man, for instance, finds it easy to write up the final report while many others find it a frightening chore. At the same time, however, he finds it rather difficult and unrewarding to think through the report and face up to the hard decisions. He is, in other words, more effective as a staff thinker who organizes and lays out the problems than as the decision-maker who takes command responsibility.

One can know about oneself that one usually does a good job working alone on a project from start to finish. One can know that one does, as a rule, quite well in negotiations, particularly emotional ones such as negotiating a union contract. But at the same time, one also knows whether one's predictions what the union will ask for have usually been correct or not.

These are not the things most people have in mind when they talk about the strengths or weaknesses of a man. They usually mean knowledge of a discipline or talent in an art. But temperament is also a factor in accomplishment and a big one. An adult usually knows quite a bit about his own temperament. To be effective he builds on what he knows he can do and does it the way he has found out he works best.

Unlike everything else discussed in this book so far, making strength productive is as much an attitude as it is a practice. But it can be improved with practice. If one disciplines oneself to ask about one's associates – subordinates as well as superiors – 'What can this man do?' rather than 'What can he not do?', one soon will acquire the attitude of looking for strengths and of using strength. And eventually one will learn to ask this question of oneself.

In every area of effectiveness within an organization, *one feeds the opportunities and starves the problem.* Nowhere is this more important than in respect to people. The effective executive looks upon people including himself as an opportunity. He knows that only strength produces results. Weakness only produces headaches – and the absence of weakness produces nothing.

He knows, moreover, that the standard of any human group is set by the performance of the leaders. And he, therefore, never allows leadership performance to be based on anything but true strength.

In sports we have long learned that the moment a new record is set every athlete all over the world acquires a new dimension of accomplishment. For years no one could run the mile in less than four minutes. Suddenly Roger Bannister broke through the old record. And soon many runners were approaching yesterday's record, while new leaders began to break through the four-minute barrier.

In human affairs, in other words, the distance between the leaders and the average is a constant. If leadership performance is high, the average will go up. The effective executive knows that it is easier to raise the performance of one leader than it is to raise the performance of a whole mass. He therefore makes sure that he puts into the leadership position, into the standard-setting, the performance-making position, the man who has the strength to do the outstanding, the pace-setting job. This always requires focus on the one strength of a man and dismissal of weaknesses as irrelevant unless they hamper the full deployment of the available strength.

The task of an executive is not to change human beings. Rather, as the Bible tells us in the Parable of the Talents, the task is to multiply performance capacity of the whole by putting to use whatever strength, whatever health, whatever aspiration there is in individuals.

5

First Things First

If there is any one 'secret' of effectiveness, it is concentration. Effective executives do first things first and they do one thing at a time.

The need to concentrate is grounded both in the nature of the executive job and in the nature of man.

Several reasons for this should already be apparent:

There are always more important contributions to be made than there is time available to make them. Any analysis of executive contributions comes up with an embarrassing richness of important tasks; and any analysis of executives' time discloses an embarrassing scarcity of time available for the work that really contributes. No matter how well an executive manages his time, the greater part of it will still not be his own. Therefore, there is always a time deficit.

The more an executive focuses on upward contribution, the more will he require fairly big continuous chunks of time. The more he switches from being busy to achieving results, the more will he shift to sustained efforts – efforts which require a fairly big quantum of time to bear fruit. Yet to get even that half-day or those two weeks of really productive time requires self-discipline and an iron determination to say 'No'.

Similarly, the more an executive works at making strengths productive, the more will he become conscious of the need to concentrate the human strengths available to him on major opportunities. This is the only way to get results.

But concentration is dictated also by the fact that most of us find it hard enough to do well even one thing at a time, let alone two. Mankind is indeed capable of doing an amazingly wide diversity of things; humanity is a 'multi-purpose tool'. But the way to apply productively mankind's great range is to bring to bear a large number of individual capabilities on one task. It is concentration in which all faculties are focused on one achievement.

We rightly consider keeping many balls in the air a circus stunt. Yet even the juggler does it only for ten minutes or so.

If he were to try doing it longer, he would soon drop all the balls.

People do, of course, differ. Some do their best work when doing two tasks in parallel at the same time, thus providing a change of pace. This presupposes, however, that they give each of the two tasks the minimum quantum needed to get anything done. But few people, I think, can perform with excellence three major tasks simultaneously.

There was Mozart, of course. He could, it seems, work on several compositions at the same time, all of them masterpieces. But he is the only known exception. The other prolific composers of the first rank – Bach, for instance, Handel, or Haydn, or Verdi – composed one work at a time. They did not begin the next until they had finished the preceding one, or until they had stopped work on it for the time being and put it away in the drawer. Executives can hardly assume that they are 'executive Mozarts'.

Concentration is necessary precisely because the executive faces so many tasks clamouring to be done. For doing one thing at a time means doing it fast. The more one can concentrate time, effort, and resources, the greater the number and diversity of tasks one can actually perform.

No chief executive of any business I have ever known accomplished as much as the recently retired head of a pharmaceutical firm. When he took over, the company was small and operated in one country only. When he retired eleven years later, the company had become a world-wide leader.

This man worked for the first years exclusively on research direction, research programme, and research personnel. The organization had never been a leader in research and had usually been tardy even as a follower. The new chief executive was not a scientist. But he realized that the company had to stop doing five years later what the leaders had pioneered five years before. It had to decide on its own direction. As a result, it moved within five years into a leadership position in two new important fields. The chief executive then turned to building an international company – years after the leaders, such as the old Swiss pharmaceutical houses, had established themselves as leaders all over the world. Carefully analysing drug consumption, he concluded that health insurance and government health services act as the main stimuli to drug demand. By timing his entry into a new country to coincide with a major expansion of its health services he managed to start big in countries where his company had never been before, and without having to take away markets from the well-entrenched, international drug firms.

The last five years of his tenure he concentrated on working out the strategy appropriate to the nature of modern health care, which is fast becoming a 'public utility' in which public bodies such as governments, non-profit hospitals, and semi-public agencies (such as Blue Cross in the United States) pay the bills although an individual, the physician, decides on the actual purchase. Whether his strategy will work out, it is too early to say – it was only perfected in 1965, shortly before he retired. But his is the only one of the major drug companies that, to my knowledge, has even thought about strategy, pricing, marketing, and the relationships of the industry world-wide.

It is unusual for any one chief executive to do one task of such magnitude during his entire tenure. Yet this man did three – in addition to building a strong, well-staffed, world-wide organization. He did this by single-minded concentration on one task at a time.

This is the 'secret' of those people who 'do so many things' and apparently so many difficult things. They do only one at a time. As a result, they need much less time in the end than the rest of us.

The people who get nothing done often work a great deal harder. In the first place, they under-estimate the time for any one task. They always expect that everything will go right. Yet, as every executive knows, nothing ever goes right. The unexpected always happens – the unexpected is indeed the only thing one can confidently expect. And almost never is it a pleasant surprise. Effective executives therefore allow a fair margin of time beyond what is actually needed. In the second place, the typical (that is, the more or less ineffectual) executive tries to hurry – and that only puts him further behind. Effective executives do not race. They set an easy pace but keep going steadily. Finally, the typical executive tries to do several things at once. Therefore, he never has the minimum time quantum for any of the tasks in his programme. If any one of them runs into trouble, his entire programme collapses.

Effective executives know that they have to get many things

done – and done effectively. Therefore, they concentrate – their own time and energy as well as that of their organization – on doing one thing at a time, and on doing first things first.

II. Sloughing Off Yesterday

The first rule for the concentration of executive efforts is to slough off the past that has ceased to be productive. Effective executives periodically review their work programmes – and those of their associates – and ask: 'If we did not already do this, would we go into it *now*?' And unless the answer is an unconditional 'Yes' they drop the activity or curtail it sharply. At the least, they make sure that no more resources are being invested in the no longer productive past. And those first-class resources, especially those scarce resources of human strength which are engaged in these tasks of yesterday, are immediately pulled out and put to work on the opportunities of tomorrow.

Executives, whether they like it or not, are forever bailing out the past. This is inevitable. Today is always the result of actions and decisions taken yesterday. Man, however, whatever his title or rank, cannot foresee the future. Yesterday's actions and decisions, no matter how courageous or wise they may have been, inevitably become today's problems, crises, and stupidities. Yet it is the executive's specific job – whether he works in government, in a business or in any other institution – to commit today's resources to the future. This means that every executive forever has to spend time, energy and ingenuity on patching up or bailing out the actions and decisions of yesterday, whether his own or those of his predecessors. In fact this always takes up more hours of his day than any other task.

But one can at least try to limit one's servitude to the past by cutting out those inherited activities and tasks that have ceased to promise results.

No one has much difficulty getting rid of the total failures. They liquidate themselves. Yesterday's successes, however, always linger on long beyond their productive life.

Even more dangerous are the activities which should do well and which, for some reason or other, do not produce. These tend to become, as I have explained elsewhere* 'investments in

* *Managing for Results* (New York: Harper & Row; London, Heinemann, 1964).

managerial ego' and sacred. Yet unless they are pruned, and pruned ruthlessly, they drain the life blood from an organization. It is always the most capable people who are wasted in the futile attempt to obtain for the investment in managerial ego the success it 'deserves'.

Every organization is highly susceptible to these twin diseases. But they are particularly prevalent in government. Government programmes and activities age just as fast as the programmes and activities of other institutions. Yet they are not only conceived as eternal; they are welded into the structure through civil-service rules and immediately become vested interests, with their own spokesmen in the legislature.

This was not too dangerous when government was small and played a minor role in social life as it did up till 1914. Today's government, however, cannot afford the diversion of its energies and resources into yesterday. Yet, at a guess, at least half the bureaus and agencies of the Federal government of the United States either regulate what no longer needs regulation – for example the Interstate Commerce Commission whose main efforts are still directed toward protecting the public from a monopoly of the railroads that disappeared thirty years ago. Or they are directed, as is most of the farm programme, toward investment in politicians' egos and toward efforts that should have had results but never achieved them.

There is serious need for a new principle of effective administration under which every act, every agency, and every programme of government is conceived as temporary and as expiring automatically after a fixed number of years – maybe ten – unless specifically prolonged by new legislation following careful outside study of the programme, its results, and its contributions.

President Johnson in 1965–6 ordered such a study for all government agencies and their programmes, adapting the 'programme review' which Secretary McNamara had developed to rid the Defence Department of the barnacles of obsolete and unproductive work. This is a good first step, and badly needed. But it will not produce results as long as we maintain the traditional assumption that all programmes last for ever unless proven to have outlived their usefulness. The assumption should rather be that all programmes outlive their usefulness fast and should be scrapped unless proven productive and necessary.

Otherwise modern government while increasingly smothering society under rules, regulations, and forms, will itself be smothered in its own fat.

But while government is particularly endangered by organizational obesity, no organization is immune to the disease. The businessman in the large corporation who complains the loudest about bureaucracy in government may encourage in his own company the growth of 'controls' which do not control anything, the proliferation of studies that are only a cover-up for his own unwillingness to face up to a decision, the inflation of all kinds of staffs for all kinds of research or 'relations'. And he himself may waste his own time and that of his key people on the obsolescent product of yesterday while starving tomorrow's successful product. The academician who is loudest in his denunciation of the horrible wastefulness of big business may fight the hardest in the faculty meeting to prolong the life of an obsolescent subject area by making it a required course.

The executive who wants to be effective and who wants his organization to be effective always polices all programmes, all activities, all tasks. He always asks: 'Is this still worth doing?' And if it isn't, he gets rid of it so as to be able to concentrate on the few tasks that, if done with excellence, will really make a difference in the results of his own job and in the performance of his organization.

Above all, the effective executive will slough off an old activity before he starts on a new one. This is necessary in order to keep organizational 'weight control'. Without it, the organization soon loses shape, cohesion, and manageability. Social organizations need to stay lean and muscular as much as biological organism.

But also, as every executive has learned, nothing new is easy. It always gets into trouble. Unless one has therefore built into the new endeavour the means for bailing it out when it runs into heavy weather, one condemns it to failure from the start. The only effective means for bailing out the new are people who have proven their capacity to perform. Such people are always already busier than they should be. Unless one relieves one of them of his present burden, one cannot expect him to take on the new task.

The alternative – to 'hire in' new people for new tasks – is too risky. One hires new people to expand an already established and smoothly running activity. But one starts something new with people of tested and proven strength, that is with veterans. Every new task is such a gamble – even if other firms have done the same job many times before – that an experienced and effective executive will not, if humanly possible, add to it the additional gamble of hiring an outsider to take charge. He has learned the hard way how many men who looked like geniuses when they worked elsewhere, show up as miserable failures six months after they have started working 'for us'.

An organization needs to bring in fresh people with fresh points of view fairly often. If it only promotes from within it soon becomes inbred and eventually sterile. But if at all possible, one does not bring in the newcomers where the risk is exorbitant, that is into the top executive positions or into leadership of an important new activity. One brings them in just below the top and into an activity that is already defined and reasonably well understood.

Systematic sloughing off of the old is the one and only way to force the new. There is no lack of ideas in any organization I know. 'Creativity' is not our problem. But few organizations ever get going on their own good ideas. Everybody is much too busy on the tasks of yesterday. Putting all programmes and activities regularly on trial for their lives, and getting rid of those that cannot prove their productivity, works wonders in stimulating creativity even in the most hidebound bureaucracy.

Du Pont has been doing so much better than any other of the world's large chemical companies, largely because Du Pont abandons a product or a process *before* it begins to decline. It does not invest scarce resources of people and money into defending yesterday. Most other businesses, however, inside and outside the chemical industry, are run on different principles, viz: 'There'll always be a market for an efficient buggy-whip plant,' and, 'This product built this company and it's our duty to maintain for it the market it deserves.'

It's those other companies, however, which send their executives to seminars on creativity and which complain about the absence of new products. Du Pont is much too busy making and selling new products to do either.

The need to slough off the outworn old to make possible the productive new is universal. It is reasonably certain that we would still have stage-coaches – nationalized, to be sure, heavily subsidized, and with a fantastic research programme to 'retrain the horse' – had there been ministries of transportation around 1825.

III. Priorities and Posteriorities

There are always more productive tasks for tomorrow than there is time to do them and more opportunities than there are capable people to take care of them – not to mention the always abundant problems and crises.

A decision therefore has to be made which tasks deserve priority and which are of less importance. The only question is which will make the decision – the executive or the pressures. But somehow the tasks will be adjusted to the available time and the opportunities will become available only to the extent to which capable people are around to take charge of them.

If the pressures rather than the executive are allowed to make the decision, the important tasks will predictably be sacrificed. Typically, there will then be no time for the most time-consuming part of any task, the conversion of decision into action. No task is completed until it has become part of organizational action and behaviour. This almost always means that no task is complete unless other people have taken it on as their own, have accepted new ways of doing old things, or the necessity for doing something new, and have otherwise made the executive's 'completed' project their own daily routine. If this is slighted because there is no time, then all the work and effort have been for nothing. Yet this is the invariable result of the executive's failure to concentrate and to impose priorities.

Another predictable result of leaving control of priorities to the pressures is that the work of top management does not get done at all. That is always postponable work, for it does not try to solve yesterday's crises but to make a different tomorrow. And the pressures always favour yesterday. In particular a top group which lets itself be controlled by the pressures will slight the one job no one else can do. It will not pay attention to the outside of the organization. It will therefore lose touch with the only reality, the only area in which there are results. For the pressures always favour what goes on inside. They always favour what has happened over the future, the crisis over the opportunity, the immediate and visible over the real, and the urgent over the relevant.

The job is, however, not to set priorities. That is easy. Everybody can do it. The reason why so few executives concentrate is the difficulty of setting 'posteriorities' – that is, deciding what tasks not to tackle – and of sticking to the decision.

Most executives have learned that what one postpones, one actually abandons. A good many of them suspect that there is nothing less desirable than to take up later a project one has postponed when it first came up. The timing is almost bound to be wrong, and timing is a most important element in the success of any effort. To do five years later what it would have been smart to do five years earlier, is almost a sure recipe for frustration and failure.

Outside of Victorian novels, happiness does not come to the marriage of two people who almost got married at age 21 and who then, at age 38, both widowed, find each other again. If married at age 21, these people might have had an opportunity to grow up together. But in seventeen years both have changed, grown apart, and developed their own ways.

The man who wanted to become a doctor as a youth but was forced to go into business instead, and who now, at age 50 and successful, goes back to his first love and enrolls in medical school, is not likely to finish, let alone to become a successful physician. He may succeed if he has extraordinary motivation, such as a strong religious drive to become a medical missionary. But otherwise he will find the discipline and rote learning of medical school irksome beyond endurance, and medical practice itself humdrum and a bore.

The merger which looked so right six or seven years earlier, but had to be postponed because one company's president refused to serve under the other, is rarely still the right 'marriage' for either side when the stiff-necked executive has finally retired.

That one actually abandons what one postpones makes executives, however, shy from postponing anything altogether. They know that this or that task is not a first priority, but giving it a posteriority is risky. What one has relegated may turn out to be the competitor's triumph. There is no guarantee that the policy area a politician or an administrator has decided to slight may not explode into the hottest and most dangerous political issue.

Neither President Eisenhower nor President Kennedy, for instance, wanted to give high priority to civil rights. And

President Johnson most definitely considered Vietnam – and foreign affairs altogether – a posteriority when he came to power. (This, in large measure, explains the violent reaction against him on the part of the liberals who had supported his original priority choice of the War on Poverty, when events forced him to change his priority schedule.)

Setting a posteriority is also unpleasant. Every posteriority is somebody else's top priority.

It is much easier to draw up a nice list of top priorities and then to hedge by trying to do 'just a little bit' of everything else as well. This makes everybody happy. The only drawback is, of course, that nothing whatever gets done.

A great deal could be said about the analysis of priorities. The most important thing about priorities and posteriorities is, however, not intelligent analysis but courage.

Courage rather than analysis dictates the truly important rules for identifying priorities:

- pick the future as against the past;
- focus on opportunity rather than on problem;
- choose your own direction – rather than climb on the bandwagon; and
- aim high, aim for something that will make a difference, rather than for something that is 'safe' and easy to do.

A good many studies of research scientists have shown that achievement (at least below the genius level of an Einstein, a Niels Bohr, or a Max Planck) depends less on ability in doing research than on the courage to go after opportunity. Those research scientists who pick their projects according to the greatest likelihood of quick success, rather than according to the challenge of the problem, are unlikely to achieve distinction. They may turn out a great many footnotes, but neither a law of physics nor a new concept is likely to be named after them. Achievement goes to the people who pick their research priorities by the opportunity and who consider other criteria only as qualifiers rather than as determinants.

In business similarly, the successful companies are not those that work at developing new products for their existing line but those that aim at innovating new technologies or new businesses.

For as a rule it is just as risky, just as arduous, and just as uncertain to do something small that is new, as it is to do something big that is new. It is more productive to convert an opportunity into results than to solve a problem – which only restores the equilibrium of yesterday.

Priorities and posteriorities always have to be reconsidered and revised in the light of realities. No American president, for instance, has been allowed by events to stick to his original list of priority tasks. In fact accomplishing one's priority tasks always changes the priorities and posteriorities themselves.

The effective executive does not, in other words, truly commit himself beyond the *one* task he concentrates on right now. Then he reviews the situation and picks the next one task that now comes first.

Concentration, that is the courage to impose on time and events his own decision as to what really matters and comes first, is the executive's only hope of becoming master of time and events instead of their whipping boy.

6

The Elements of Decision-making

Decision-making is only one of the tasks of an executive. It usually takes but a small fraction of his time. But to make decisions is the *specific* executive task. Decision-making therefore deserves special treatment in a discussion of the effective executive. Only executives make decisions. Indeed to be expected, by virtue of position or knowledge, to make decisions that have significant impact on the entire organization, its performance and results, defines the executive.

Effective executives, therefore, make effective decisions.

They make these decisions as a systematic process with clearly defined elements and in a distinct sequence of steps. But this process bears amazingly little resemblance to what so many books today present as 'decision-making'.

Effective executives do not make a great many decisions. They concentrate on the important ones. They try to think through what is strategic and generic, rather than solve problems. They try to make the few important decisions on the highest level of conceptual understanding. They try to find the constants in a situation. They are, therefore, not overly impressed by speed in decision-making. Rather they consider virtuosity in manipulating a great many variables a symptom of sloppy thinking. They want to know what the decision is all about and what the underlying realities are which it has to satisfy. They want impact rather than technique, they want to be sound rather than clever.

Effective executives know when a decision has to be based on principle and when it should be made on the merits of the case and pragmatically. They know that the trickiest decision is that between the right and the wrong compromise and have learned to tell one from the other. They know that the most time-consuming step in the process is not making the decision but putting it into effect. Unless a decision has 'degenerated into work' it is not a decision; it is at best a good intention. This means that, while the effective decision itself is based on the highest level of conceptual understanding, the action to carry it out should be as close as possible to the working level and as simple as possible.

I. Two Case Studies in Decision-making

The least-known of the great American business-builders, Theodore Vail, was perhaps the most effective decision-maker in United States business history. As president of the Bell Telephone System from just before 1910 till the mid-1920s, Vail built the organization into the largest private business in the world and into one of the most prosperous growth companies.

That the telephone system is privately owned is taken for granted in the United States. But the part of the North American continent that the Bell System serves (the United States and the two most populous Canadian provinces, Quebec and Ontario) is the only developed area in the world in which telecommunications are not owned by government. The Bell System is also the only public utility that has shown itself capable of risk-taking leadership and rapid growth, even though it has a monopoly in a vital area and has achieved saturation of its original market.

The explanation is not luck, or 'American conservatism'. The explanation lies in four strategic decisions Vail made in the course of almost twenty years.

Vail saw early that a telephone system had to do something distinct and different to remain in private ownership and under autonomous management. All over Europe governments were running the telephone without much trouble or risk. To attempt to keep Bell private by defending it against government take-overs would be a delaying action only. Moreover, a purely defensive posture could only be self-defeating. It would paralyse management's imagination and energies. A policy was needed which would make Bell, as a private company, stand for the interest of the public more forcefully than any government agency could. This led to Vail's early decision that the business of the Bell Telephone Company must be anticipation and satisfaction of the service requirements of the public.

'Our business is service' became the Bell commitment as soon as Vail took over. At the time, shortly after the turn of the century, this was heresy. But Vail was not content to preach that it was the business of the company to give service, and that it was the job of management to make service possible and profitable. He saw to it that the yardsticks throughout the system by which managers and their operations were judged, measured service fulfilment rather than profit performance. Managers are responsible for service results. It is then the job of top management to organize and finance the company so as to make the best service also result in optimal financial rewards.

Vail, at about the same time, realized that a nation-wide communications monopoly could not be a free enterprise in the traditional sense, that is, unfettered private business. He recognized public regulation as the only alternative to government ownership. Effective, honest, and principled public regulation was, therefore, in the interest of the Bell System and vital to its preservation.

Public regulation, while by no means unknown in the United States, was by and large impotent when Vail reached this conclusion. Business opposition, powerfully aided by the Courts, had drawn the teeth of the laws on on the statute books. The commissions themselves were understaffed and underfinanced and had become sinecures for third-rate and often venal political hacks.

Vail set the Bell Telephone System the objective of making regulation effective. He gave this as their main task to the heads of each of the affiliated regional telephone companies. It was their job to rejuvenate the regulatory bodies and to innovate concepts of regulation and of rate-making that would be fair and equitable and would protect the public, while at the same time permitting the Bell System to do its job. The affiliated-company presidents were the group from which the Bell top management was recruited. This ensured that positive attitudes toward regulation permeated the entire company.

Vail's third decision led to the establishment of one of the most successful scientific laboratories in industry, the Bell Laboratories. Again, Vail started out with the need to make a private monopoly viable. Only this time he asked: 'How can one make such a monopoly truly competitive?' Obviously it was not subject to the normal competition from another supplier who offers the purchaser the same product or one supplying the same want. And yet without competition such a monopoly would rapidly become rigid and incapable of growth and change.

But even in a monopoly, Vail concluded, one can organize the future to compete with the present. In a technical industry such as telecommunications, the future lies in better and different technologies. The Bell Laboratories which grew out of this insight were by no means the first industrial laboratory, not even in the United States. But they were the first industrial research institution that was deliberately designed to make obsolete the present, no matter how profitable and efficient.

When Bell Labs took its final form, during the World War I period, this was a breath-taking innovation in industry. Even today few businessmen understand that research, to be productive, has to be the 'disorganizer', the creator of a different future and the enemy of today. In most industrial laboratories, 'defensive research' aimed at perpetuating today, predominates. But from the very beginning, the Bell Labs never undertook defensive research.

The last ten or fifteen years have proven how sound Vail's concept was. Bell Labs first extended telephone technology so that the entire North American continent became one automated switchboard. It then extended the Bell System's reach into areas never dreamed of by Vail and his generation, e.g. the transmission of television programmes, the transmission of computer data – in the last few years the most rapidly growing communications area – and the communications satellites. The scientific and technical developments that make possible these new transmission systems originated largely in the Bell Labs, whether they were scientific theory such as mathematical information theory, new products and processes such as the transistor, or computer logic and design.

Finally, toward the end of his career, in the early twenties, Vail invented the mass capital market – again to ensure survival of the Bell System as a private business.

Industries are more commonly taken over by government because they fail to attract the capital they need than because of socialism. Failure to attract the needed capital was a main reason why the European railroads were taken over by government between 1860 and 1920. Inability to attract the needed capital to modernize certainly played a big part in the nationalization of the coal mines and of the electric power industry in Great Britain. It was one of the major reasons for the nationalization of the electric power industry on the European continent in the inflationary period after World War I. The electric power companies, unable to raise their rates to offset currency depreciation, could no longer attract capital for modernization and expansion.

Whether Vail saw the problem in its full breadth, the record does not show. But he clearly saw that the Bell Telephone System needed tremendous sums of capital in a dependable, steady supply which could not be obtained from the then existing capital markets. The other public utilities, especially the electric power companies, tried to make investment in their securities attractive to the one and only mass participant visible in the twenties: the speculator. They built holding companies that gave the common shares of the parent company speculative leverage and appeal, while the needs of the operating businesses were satisfied primarily by debt money raised from traditional sources such as insurance companies. Vail realized that this was not a sound capital foundation. The AT & T common stock which he designed to solve his problem, in the early twenties, had nothing in common with the speculative shares except legal form. It was to be a security for the general public, the 'Aunt Sallys' of the emerging middle class, who could put something aside for investment, but had not enough capital to take much risk. Vail's AT & T common, with its almost-guaranteed dividend, was close enough to a fixed interest-bearing obligation for widows and orphans to buy it. At the same time, it was a common share so that it held out the promise of capital appreciation and of protection in inflation.

When Vail designed this financial instrument, the 'Aunt Sally' type of investor did not, in effect, exist. The middle class that had enough money to buy any kind of common share had only recently emerged. It was still following older habits of investment in savings banks, insurance policies, and mortgages. Those who ventured further went into the speculative stock market of the twenties – where they had no business to be at all. Vail did not, of course, invent the 'Aunt Sallys'. But he made them into investors and mobilized their savings for their benefit as well as for that of the Bell System. This alone has enabled the Bell System to raise the hundreds of billions of dollars it has had to invest over the last half-century. All this time AT & T common has remained the foundation of investment planning for the middle classes in the United States and Canada.

Vail again provided this idea with its own means of execution. Rather than depend on Wall Street, the Bell System has all these years been its own banker and underwriter. And Vail's principal assistant on financial design, Walter Gifford, was made chief officer of the Bell System and became Vail's successor.

The decisions Vail reached were, of course, peculiar to his problems and those of his company. But the basic thinking behind them characterizes the truly effective decision.

The example of Alfred P. Sloan, Jr., shows this clearly.* Sloan, who in General Motors designed and built the world's largest manufacturing enterprise, took over as head of a big business in 1922, when Vail's career was drawing to its close. He was a very different man, as his was a very different time. And yet the decision for which Sloan is best remembered, the decentralized organization structure of General Motors, is of the same kind as the major decisions Theodore Vail had made somewhat earlier for the Bell Telephone System.

As Sloan has recounted in his recent book, *My Years with General Motors*† the company he took over in 1922 was a loose federation of almost independent chieftains. Each of these men ran a unit which a few short years before had still been his own company – and each ran it as if it were still his own company.

There were two traditional ways of handling such a situation. One was to get rid of the strong independent men after they had sold out their business. This was the way in which John D. Rockefeller had put together the Standard Oil Trust, and J. P. Morgan, only a few years before Sloan, had put together United States Steel. The alternative was to leave the former owners in their commands with a minimum of interference from the new central office. It was 'anarchy tempered by stock options' in which, it was hoped, their own financial interest would make the chieftains act for the best interests of the entire business. Durant, the founder of General Motors and Sloan's predecessor, Pierre Du Pont, had followed this route. When Sloan took over,

* Business examples are chosen here because they are still taken in a small enough compass to be easily comprehended – whereas most decisions in government policy require far too much explanation of background, history, and politics. At the same time, these are large enough examples to show structure. But decisions in government, the military, the hospital, or the university exemplify the same concepts as the next sections of this and the following chapter will demonstrate.

† New York, Doubleday, 1964.

however, the refusal of these strong and self-willed men to work together had all but destroyed the company.

Sloan realized that this was not the peculiar and short-term problem of the company just created through merger, but a generic problem of big business. The big business, Sloan saw, needs unity of direction and central control. It needs its own top management with real powers. But it equally needs energy, enthusiasm, and strength in operations. The operating managers have to have the freedom to do things their own way. They have to have responsibility and the authority that goes with it. They have to have scope to show what they can do, and they have to get recognition for performance. This, Sloan apparently saw right away, becomes even more important as a company gets older and as it has to depend on developing strong, independent, performing executives from within.

Everyone before Sloan had seen the problem as one of personalities, to be solved through a struggle for power from which one man would emerge victorious. Sloan saw it as a constitutional problem to be solved through a new structure; decentralization which balances local autonomy in operations with central control of direction and policy.

How effective this solution has been shows perhaps best by contrast: that is in the one area where General Motors has not had extraordinary results. General Motors, at least since the mid-thirties, has done poorly in anticipating and understanding the political temper of the American people and the direction and policies of American government. This is the one area, however, where there has been no 'decentralization' in General Motors. Since 1935 or so it has been practically unthinkable for any senior GM executive to be anything but a conservative Republican.

These specific decisions – Vail's as well as Sloan's – have major features in common, even though they dealt with entirely different problems and led to highly specific solutions. They all tackled a problem at the highest conceptual level of understanding. They tried to think through what the decision was all about, and then tried to develop a principle for dealing with it. Their decisions were, in other words, strategic, rather than adaptations to the apparent needs of the moment. They all innovated. They were all highly controversial. Indeed, all five decisions went directly counter to what 'everybody knew' at the time.

Vail had actually been fired earlier by the board of the Bell System when he first was president. His concept of service as the business of the company seemed almost insane to people who 'knew' that the only purpose of a business is to make a profit. His belief that regulation was in the best interest of the company was indeed a necessity for survival, appeared hare-brained, if not immoral, to people who 'knew' that regulation was 'creeping socialism' to be fought tooth and nail. It was only years later, after 1900, when they had become alarmed – and with good reason – by the rising tide of demand for the nationalization of the telephone, that the board called Vail back. But his decision to spend money on obsoleting current processes and techniques just when they made the greatest profits for the company and to build a large research laboratory designed to this end, as well as his refusal to follow the fashion in finance and build a speculative capital structure, were equally resisted by his board as worse than eccentricity.

Similarly, Alfred Sloan's decentralization was completely unacceptable at the time and seemed to fly in the face of everything everybody 'knew'.

The acknowledged radical among American business leaders of those days was Henry Ford. But Vail's and Sloan's decisions were much too 'wild' for Ford. He was certain that the Model T, once it had been designed, was the right car for all time to come. Vail's insistence on organized self-obsolescence would have struck him as lunacy. He was equally convinced that only the tightest centralized control could produce efficiency and results. Sloan's decentralization appeared to him self-destructive weakness.

II. The Elements of the Decision-process

The truly important features of the decisions Vail and Sloan made are neither their novelty nor their controversial nature. They are:

1 the clear realization that the problem was generic and could only be solved through a decision which established a rule, a principle;

2 the definition of the specifications which the answer to the problem had to satisfy, that is, of the 'boundary conditions';

3 the thinking through what is 'right', that is, the solution which will fully satisfy the specifications *before* attention is given

to the compromises, adaptations, and concessions needed to make the decision acceptable;

4 the building into the decision of the action to carry it out;

5 the 'feedback' which tests the validity and effectiveness of the decision against the actual course of events.

These are the *elements* of the effective decision-process.

1. The first question the effective decision-maker asks is: 'Is this a generic situation or an exception? Is this something that underlies a great many occurrences? Or is the occurrence a unique event that needs to be dealt with as such?' The generic always has to be answered through a rule, a principle. The exceptional can only be handled as such and as it comes.

Strictly speaking, one might distinguish between four, rather than between two, different types of occurrences.

There is first the truly generic of which the individual occurrence is only a symptom.

Most of the problems that come up in the course of the executive's work are of this nature. Inventory decisions in a business, for instance, are not 'decisions'. They are adaptations. The problem is generic. This is even more likely to be true of events within production.

Typically, a product control and engineering group will handle many hundreds of problems in the course of a month. Yet, whenever these are analysed, the great majority prove to be just symptoms – and manifestations of underlying basic situations. The individual process control engineer or production engineer who works in one part of the plant usually cannot see this. He might have a few problems each month with the couplings in the pipes that carry steam or hot liquids. But only when the total workload of the group over several months is analysed does the generic problem appear. Then one sees that temperatures or pressures have become too great for the existing equipment and that the couplings, holding different lines together, need to be redesigned for greater loads. Until this is done, process control will spend a tremendous amount of time fixing leaks without ever getting control of the situation.

Then there is the problem which, while a unique event for the individual institution, is actually generic.

The company that receives an offer to merge from another,

larger one, will never receive such an offer again if it accepts. This is a non-recurrent situation as far as the individual company, its board of directors, and its management are concerned. But it is, of course, a generic situation which occurs all the time. To think through whether to accept or to reject the offer requires some general rules. For these, however, one has to look to the experience of others.

Next there is the truly exceptional, the truly unique event.

The power failure that plunged into darkness the whole of North-eastern North America from the St Lawrence to Washington in November 1965 was, according to the first explanations, a truly exceptional situation. So was the thalidomide tragedy which led to the birth of so many deformed babies in the early sixties. The probability of these events, we were told, was one in ten million or one in a hundred million, and the result of concatenations of malfunctions as unlikely to recur as it is unlikely, for instance, for the chair on which I sit to disintegrate into its constituent atoms.

Truly unique events are rare, however. Whenever one appears, one has to ask: is this a true exception or only the first manifestation of a new genus?

And this, the early manifestation of a new generic problem, is the fourth and last category of events with which the decision-process deals.

We know now, for instance, that both the North-eastern power failure and the thalidomide tragedy were only the first occurrences of what, under conditions of modern power technology or of modern pharmacology, are likely to become fairly frequent malfunctions unless generic solutions are found.

All events but the truly unique require a generic solution. They require a rule, a policy, a principle. Once the right principle has been developed, all manifestations of the same generic situation can be handled pragmatically, that is, by adaptation of the rule to the concrete circumstances of the case. Truly unique events however must be treated individually. One cannot develop rules for the exceptional.

The effective decision-maker spends time to determine with which of these four situations he is dealing. He knows that he will make the wrong decision if he classifies the situation wrongly.

By far the most common mistake is to treat a generic situation as if it were a series of unique events, that is, to be pragmatic when one lacks the generic understanding and principle. This inevitably leads to frustration and futility.

This was clearly shown, I think, by the failure of most of the policies, whether domestic or foreign, of the Kennedy administration. For all the brilliance of its members, the administration achieved fundamentally only one success, in the Cuban missile crisis. Otherwise, it achieved practically nothing. The main reason was surely what its members called 'pragmatism', that is, its refusal to develop rules and principles, and its insistence on treating everything 'on its merits'. Yet it was clear to everyone, including the members of the administration, that the basic assumptions on which its policies rested, the basic assumptions of the post-war years, had become increasingly unrealistic in international as well as in domestic affairs.

Equally common is the mistake of treating a new event as if it were just another example of the old problem to which, therefore, the old rules should be applied.

This was the error that snowballed the local power failure on the New York–Ontario border into the great North-eastern blackout. The power engineers, especially in New York City, applied the right rule for a normal overload. Yet their own instruments had signalled that something quite extraordinary was going on which called for exceptional, rather than for standard, countermeasures.

By contrast, the one great triumph of President Kennedy, in the Cuban missile crisis, rested on acceptance of the challenge to think through an extraordinary, exceptional occurrence. As soon as Mr Kennedy accepted this, his own tremendous resources of intelligence and courage effectively came into play.

Almost as common is the plausible but erroneous definition of the fundamental problem. Here is one example.

Since the end of World War II the American military services have been plagued by their inability to keep highly-trained medical people in uniform. There have been dozens of studies and dozens of proposed remedies. However, all of the studies start out with the plausible hypothesis that pay is the problem – whereas the real problem lies in the traditional structure of military medicine. With its emphasis on the general practitioner, it is out of alignment with today's medical profession, which stresses the specialist. The career ladder in military medicine leads from specialization to medical and hospital administration and away from research and specialized practice. Today's young, well-trained physicians, therefore, feel that they waste their time and skill in the military service where they either have to work as general practitioners or become chairbound administrators. They want the opportunity to develop the skills and apply the practice of today's highly scientific, specialized doctor.

So far the military has not faced up to the basic decision. Are the armed services willing to settle for a second-rate medical organization staffed with people who cannot make the grade in the highly scientific, research-oriented, and highly specialized civilian profession of medicine, or are they willing and able to organize the practice of medicine within the services in ways that differ fundamentally from the organization and structure of a military service? Until the military accepts this as the real decision, its young doctors will keep on leaving as soon as they can.

Or the definition of the problem may be incomplete.

This largely explains why the American automobile industry found itself in 1966 suddenly under sharp attack for its unsafe cars – and also why the industry itself was so totally bewildered by the attack. It is simply not true that the industry has paid no attention to safety. On the contrary, it has worked hard at safer highway engineering and at driver training. That accidents are caused by unsafe roads and unsafe drivers is plausible enough. Indeed all other agencies concerned with automotive safety, from the highway police to the schools, picked the same targets for their campaigns. These campaigns have produced results. Highways built for safety have many fewer accidents; and so have safety-trained drivers. But though the ratio of accidents per thousand cars or per thousand miles driven has been going down, the total number of accidents and their severity has kept creeping up.

Long ago it should have been clear that a small percentage of drivers – drunken drivers, for instance, or the 5 per cent who are 'accident-prone' and cause three quarters or so of all accidents – are beyond the reach of driver training and can cause accidents on the safest road. Long ago it should have become clear that we have to do something about a small but significant probability of accidents that will occur despite safety laws and safety training. And this means that safe-highway and safe-driving campaigns have to be supplemented by engineering to make accidents themselves less dangerous. Where we engineered to make cars safe when used right, we also have to engineer to make cars safe when used wrong. This, however, the automobile industry failed to see.

This example shows why the incomplete explanation is often more dangerous than the totally wrong explanation. Everyone connected with safe-driving campaigns – the automobile industry, but also state highway commissioners, automobile clubs, and insurance companies – felt that to accept a probability of accidents was to condone, if not to encourage, dangerous driving – just as my grandmother's generation believed that the doctor who treated venereal diseases abetted immorality. It is this common human tendency to confuse plausibility with morality which makes the incomplete hypothesis so dangerous a mistake and so hard to correct.

The effective decision-maker, therefore, always assumes initially that the problem is generic.

He always assumes that the event that clamours for his attention is in reality a symptom. He looks for the true problem. He is not content with doctoring the symptom alone.

And if the event is truly unique, the experienced decision-maker suspects that this heralds a new underlying problem and that what appears as unique will turn out to have been simply the first manifestation of a new generic situation.

This also explains why the effective decision-maker always tries to put his solution on the highest possible conceptual level. He does not solve the immediate financing problem by issuing whatever security would be easiest to sell at the best price for the next few years. If he expects to need the capital market for the foreseeable future, he invents a new kind of investor and designs the appropriate security for a mass-capital market that does not yet exist. If he has to bring into line a flock of undisciplined but capable divisional presidents, he does not get rid of the most obstreperous ones and buys off the rest. He develops a constitutional concept of large-scale organization. If he sees his industry as necessarily monopolistic, he does not content himself with fulminating against socialism. He builds the public regulatory agency into a deliberate 'third way' between the Scylla of irresponsible private enterprise unchecked by competition and the Charybdis of equally irresponsible, indeed essentially uncontrollable, government monopoly.

One of the most obvious facts of social and political life is the longevity of the temporary. British licensing hours for taverns, for instance, French rent controls, or Washington 'temporary' government buildings, all three hastily developed in World War I to last 'a few months of temporary emergency' are still with us fifty years later. The effective decision-maker knows this. He too improvises, of course. But he asks himself every time, 'If I had to live with this for a long time, would I be willing to?' And if the answer is 'No' he keeps on working to find a more general, a more conceptual, a more comprehensive solution – one which establishes the right principle.

As a result, the effective executive does not make many decisions. But the reason is not that he takes too long in making one – in fact, a decision on principle does not, as a rule, take longer than a decision on symptoms and expediency. The effective executive does not need to make many decisions. Because he solves generic situations through a rule and policy, he can handle most events as cases under the rule, that is, by adaptation. 'A country with many laws is a country of incompetent lawyers,' says an old legal proverb. It is a country which attempts to solve every problem as a unique phenomenon, rather than as a special case under general rules of law. Similarly an executive who makes many decisions is both lazy and ineffectual.

The decision-maker also always tests for signs that something atypical, something unusual is happening; he always asks: does the explanation explain the observed events and does it explain all of them?; he always writes out what the solution is expected to make happen – make automobile accidents disappear, for instance – and then tests regularly to see if this really happens; and finally, he goes back and thinks the problem through again when he sees something atypical, when he finds phenomena his explanation does not really explain, or when the course of events deviates, even in details, from his expectations.

These are in essence the rules Hippocrates laid down for medical diagnosis well over 2,000 years ago. They are the rules for scientific observation first formulated by Aristotle and then reaffirmed by Galileo 300 years ago. These, in other words, are old, well-known, time-tested rules, rules one can learn and can systematically apply.

2. The second major element in the decision-process is clear specifications as to what the decision has to accomplish. What are the objectives the decision has to reach? What are the minimum goals it has to attain? What are the conditions it has to satisfy? In science these are known as 'boundary conditions'. A decision, to be effective, needs to satisfy the boundary conditions. It needs to be adequate to its purpose.

The more concisely and clearly boundary conditions are stated, the greater the likelihood that the decision will indeed be an effective one and will accomplish what it set out to do. Conversely, any serious shortfall in defining these boundary conditions is almost certain to make a decision ineffectual, no matter how brilliant it may seem.

'What is the minimum needed to resolve this problem?' is the form in which the boundary conditions are usually probed. 'Can our needs be satisfied,' Alfred P. Sloan presumably asked himself when he took command of General Motors in 1922, 'by removing the autonomy of the division heads?' His answer was clearly in the negative. The boundary conditions of his problem demanded strength and responsibility in the chief operating positions. This was needed as much as unity and control at the centre. The boundary conditions demanded a solution to a problem of structure, rather than an accommodation among personalities. And this in turn made his solution last.

It is not always easy to find the appropriate boundary conditions. And intelligent people do not necessarily agree on them.

> On the morning after the power blackout one New York newspaper managed to appear: *The New York Times*. It had shifted its printing operations immediately across the Hudson to Newark, New Jersey, where the power plants were functioning and where a local paper, *The Newark Evening News*, had a substantial printing plant. But instead of the million copies *The Times* management had ordered, fewer than half this number actually reached the readers. Just as *The Times* went to press (so at least goes a widely told anecdote) the executive editor and three of his assistants started arguing how to hyphenate *one*

word. This took them forty-eight minutes (so it is said) – or half of the available press time. *The Times*, the editor argued, sets a standard for written English in the United States and therefore cannot afford a grammatical mistake.

Assuming the tale to be true – and I do not vouch for it – one wonders what the management thought about the decision. But there is no doubt that given the fundamental assumptions and objectives of the executive editor, it was the right decision. His boundary conditions quite clearly were not the number of copies sold at any one morning, but the infallibility of *The Times* as a grammarian and as *Magister Americae*.

The effective executive knows that a decision that does not satisfy the boundary conditions is ineffectual and inappropriate. It may be worse indeed than a decision that satisfies the wrong boundary conditions. Both will be wrong. But one can often salvage the appropriate decision for the incorrect boundary conditions. It is still an effective decision. One cannot get anything but trouble from the decision that is inadequate to its specifications.

In fact, clear thinking about the boundary conditions is needed so that one knows when a decision has to be abandoned. There are two famous illustrations for this – one of a decision where the boundary conditions had become confused and one of a decision where they were kept so clear as to make possible immediate replacement of the outflanked decision by a new and appropriate policy.

The first example is the famous Schlieffen Plan of the German General Staff at the outbreak of World War I. This plan was meant to enable Germany to fight a war on both the eastern and the western fronts simultaneously without having to splinter her forces between East and West. To accomplish this, the Schlieffen Plan proposed to offer only token opposition to the weaker enemy, that is, to Russia, and to concentrate all forces first on a quick knockout blow against France, after which Russia would be dealt with. This, of course, implied willingness to let the Russian armies move fairly deeply into German territory at the outbreak of the war and until the decisive victory over France. But in August 1914, it became clear that the speed of the Russian armies had been underrated. The Junkers in East Prussia whose estates were overrun by the Russians set up a howl for protection.

Schlieffen himself had kept the boundary conditions clearly in his mind. But his successors were technicians rather than decision-makers and strategists. They jettisoned the basic commitment underlying the Schlieffen Plan, the commitment not to splinter the German forces. They should have dropped the Plan. Instead they kept it but made its attainment impossible. They weakened the armies in the West sufficiently to deprive their initial victories of full impact, yet did not strengthen the armies in the East sufficiently to knock out the Russians. They thereby brought about the one thing the Schlieffen Plan had been designed to prevent: a stalemate with its ensuing war of attrition in which superiority of manpower, rather than superiority of strategy, eventually had to win. Instead of a strategy, all they had from there on was confused improvisation, impassioned rhetoric, and hopes for miracles.

Contrast with this the second example, the action of Franklin D. Roosevelt when becoming president in 1933. All through his campaign Roosevelt had worked on a plan for *economic recovery*. Such a plan, in 1933, could only be built on financial conservatism and a balanced budget. Then, immediately before FDR's inauguration, the economy collapsed in the Bank Holiday. Economic policy might still have done the work economically. But it had become clear that the patient would not survive politically.

Roosevelt immediately substituted a political objective for his former economic one. He switched from recovery to reform. The new specifications called for political dynamics. This, almost automatically, meant a complete change of economic policy from one of conservatism to one of radical innovation. The boundary conditions had changed – and Roosevelt was enough of a decision-maker to know almost intuitively that this meant abandoning his original plan altogether if he wanted to have any effectiveness.

But clear thinking about the boundary conditions is needed also to identify the most dangerous of all possible decisions: the one that might – just might – work if nothing whatever goes wrong. These decisions always seem to make sense. But when one thinks through the specifications they have to satisfy, one always finds that they are essentially incompatible with each other. That such a decision might succeed is not impossible – it is merely grossly improbable. The trouble with miracles is not, after all, that they happen rarely; it is that one cannot rely on them.

A perfect example was President Kennedy's Bay of Pigs decision in 1961. One specification was clearly Castro's overthrow. But at the same time, there was another specification: not to make it appear that U.S. forces were intervening in one of the American Republics. That the second specification was rather absurd, and that no one in the whole world would have believed for one moment that the invasion was a spontaneous uprising of the Cubans, is beside the point. To the American policy-makers at the time, the appearance of non-intervention seemed a legitimate and indeed a necessary condition. But these two specifications would have been compatible with each other only if an immediate island-wide uprising against Castro would have completely paralysed the Cuban army. And this, while not impossible, was clearly not highly probable in a police-state. Either the whole idea should have been dropped or American full-scale support should have been provided to ensure success of the invasion.

It is not disrespect for President Kennedy to say that his mistake was not, as he explained, that he had 'listened to the experts'. The mistake was failure to think through clearly the boundary conditions that the decision had to satisfy, and refusal to face up to the unpleasant reality that a decision that has to satisfy two different and at bottom incompatible specifications is not a decision but a prayer for a miracle.

Yet, defining the specifications and setting the boundary conditions cannot be done on the 'facts' in any decision of importance. It always has to be done on interpretation. It is risk-taking judgment.

Everyone can make the wrong decision – in fact, everyone will sometimes make a wrong decision. But no one needs to make a decision which, on its face, falls short of satisfying the boundary conditions.

3. One has to start out with what is right rather than what is acceptable (let alone who is right) precisely because one always has to compromise in the end. But if one does not know what is right to satisfy the specifications and boundary conditions, one cannot distinguish between the right compromise and the

wrong compromise – and will end up by making the wrong compromise.

I was taught this when I started in 1944 on my first big consulting assignment, a study of the management structure and management policies of the General Motors Corporation. Alfred P. Sloan, Jr., who was then chairman and chief executive officer of the company, called me to his office at the start of my study and said: 'I shall not tell you what to study, what to write, or what conclusions to come to. This is your task. My only instruction to you is to put down what you think is right as you see it. Don't you worry about our reaction. Don't you worry about whether we will like this or dislike that. And don't you, above all, concern yourself with the compromises that might be needed to make your recommendations acceptable. There is not one executive in this company who does not know how to make every single conceivable compromise without any help from you. But he can't make the *right* compromise unless you first tell him what 'right' is.' The executive thinking through a decision might put this in front of himself in neon lights.

President Kennedy learned this lesson from the Bay of Pigs fiasco. It largely explains his triumph in the Cuban missile crisis two years later. His ruthless insistence then on thinking through what boundary conditions the decision had to satisfy gave him the knowledge of what compromise to accept (i.e. tacitly to abandon the U.S. demand for on-the-ground inspection after air reconnaissance had shown such inspection to be no longer necessary) and what to insist on, namely, the physical dismantling and return to Russia of the Soviet missiles themselves.

For there are two different kinds of compromise. One kind is expressed in the old proverb: 'Half a loaf is better than no bread.' The other kind is expressed in the story of the Judgment of Solomon, which was clearly based on the realization that 'half a baby is worse than no baby at all'. In the first instance, the boundary conditions are still being satisfied. The purpose of bread is to provide food, and half a loaf is still food. Half a baby, however, does not satisfy the boundary conditions. For half a baby is not half of a living and growing child. It is a corpse in two pieces.

It is fruitless and a waste of time to worry about what is acceptable and what one had better not say so as not to evoke resistance.

The things one worries about never happen. And objections and difficulties no one thought about suddenly turn out to be almost insurmountable obstacles. One gains nothing in other words by starting out with the question: 'What is acceptable?' And in the process of answering it, one gives away the important things, as a rule, and loses any chance to come up with an effective, let alone with the right, answer.

4. Converting the decision into action is the fourth major element in the decision-process. While thinking through the boundary conditions is the most difficult step in decision-making, converting the decision into effective action is usually the most time-consuming one. Yet a decision will not become effective unless the action commitments have been built into the decision from the start.

In fact, no decision has been made unless carrying it out in specific steps has become someone's work assignment and responsibility. Until then, there are only good intentions.

This is the trouble with so many policy statements, especially of business. They contain no action commitment. To carry them out is no one's specific work and responsibility. No wonder that the people in the organization tend to view these statements cynically if not as declarations of what top management is really not going to do.

Converting a decision into action requires answering several distinct questions: Who has to know of this decision? What action has to be taken? Who is to take it?; and What does the action have to be so that the people who have to do it *can* do it? The first and the last of these are too often overlooked – with dire results.

A story that has become a legend among operational researchers illustrates the importance of the question 'Who has to know?' A major manufacturer of industrial equipment decided several years ago to discontinue one model. For years it had been standard equipment on a line of machine tools, many of which were still in use. It was, therefore, decided to sell the model to present owners of the old equipment for another three years as a replacement, and then to stop making and selling it. Orders for this particular model had been going down for a good many years. But they shot up as former customers reordered against the day when the model would no longer be available. No one had, however, asked, 'Who needs to know of this decision?' Therefore nobody informed the clerk in the purchasing department who was in charge of buying the parts from which the model itself was being assembled. His instructions were to buy parts in a given ratio to current sales – and the instructions remained unchanged. When the time came to discontinue further production of the model, the company had in its warehouse enough parts for another eight to ten years of production, parts that had to be written off at a considerable loss.

The action must also be appropriate to the capacities of the people who have to carry it out.

A chemical company found itself, in recent years, with fairly large amounts of blocked currency in two West African countries. It decided that to protect this money, it had to invest it locally in businesses which would contribute to the local economy, would not require imports from abroad, and would, if successful, be the kind that could be sold to local investors if and when currency remittances became possible again. To establish these businesses, the company developed a simple chemical process to preserve a tropical fruit which is a staple crop in both countries and which, up till then, had suffered serious spoilage in transit to its Western markets.

The business was a success in both countries. But in one country the local manager set the business up in such a manner that it required highly skilled and, above all, technically trained management of the kind not easily available in West Africa. In the other country the local manager thought through the capacities of the people who would eventually have to run the business and worked hard at making both process and business simple and at staffing from the start with nationals of the country right up to the top.

A few years later it became possible again to transfer currency from these two countries. But though the business flourished, no buyer could be found for it in the first country. No one available locally had the necessary managerial and technical skills. The business had to be liquidated at a loss. In the other country so many local entrepreneurs were eager to buy the business that the company repatriated its original investment with a substantial profit.

The process and the business built on it were essentially the same in both places. But in the first country no one had asked: 'What kind of people do we have available to make this decision effective? And what can they do?' As a result, the decision itself became frustrated.

All this becomes doubly important when people have to change behaviour, habits or attitudes if a decision is to become effective action. Here one has to make sure not only that responsibility for the action is clearly assigned and that the people responsible are capable of doing the needful. One has to make sure that their measurements, their standards for accomplishment, and their incentives are changed simultaneously. Otherwise, the people will get caught in a paralysing internal emotional conflict.

Theodore Vail's decision that the business of the Bell System was service might have remained dead letter but for the yardsticks of service performance which he designed to measure managerial performance. Bell managers were used to being measured by the profitability of their units, or at the least, by cost. The new yardsticks made them accept rapidly the new objectives.

In sharp contrast is the recent failure of a brilliant chairman and chief executive to make effective a new organization structure and new objectives in an old, large, and proud American company. Everyone agreed that the changes were needed. The company, after many years as leader of its industry, showed definite signs of ageing; in almost all major fields newer, smaller, and more aggressive competitors were outflanking it. But to gain acceptance for the new ideas, the chairman promoted the most prominent spokesmen of the old school into the most visible and best-paid positions – especially into three new executive vice-presidencies. This meant only one thing to the people in the company: 'They don't really mean it'.

If the greatest rewards are given for behaviour contrary to that which the new course of action requires, then everyone will conclude that this contrary behaviour is what the people at the top really want and are going to reward.

Not everyone can do what Vail did and build the execution of his decisions into the decision itself. But everyone can think what action commitments a specific decision requires, what work assignments follow from it, and what people are available to carry it out.

5. Finally, a feedback has to be built into the decision to provide a continuous testing, against actual events, of the expectations that underlie the decisions.

Decisions are made by men. Men are fallible; at their best their works do not last long. Even the best decision has a high probability of being wrong. Even the most effective one eventually becomes obsolete.

If this needs documentation, the Vail and Sloan decisions supply it. Despite their imagination and daring only one of Vail's decisions, the decision that service was the business of the Bell System, is still valid today and applicable in the form in which he worked it out. The investment character of the AT & T common share had to be drastically changed in the nineteen-fifties in response to the emergence of the institutional investors-pension trusts and mutual funds – as the new channels through which the middle class invests. While Bell Labs has maintained its dominant position, the new scientific and technological developments – especially in space technology and in such devices as the laser – have made it reasonably clear that no communications company, no matter how large, can any longer hope to provide by its own means all its own technological and scientific needs. At the same time, the development of technology has made it probable – for the first time in 75 years – that new processes of telecommunications will seriously compete with the telephone, and that in major communications fields, e.g. information and data communication, no single communications medium can maintain dominance, let alone the monopoly which Bell has had for voice communications over distance. And while regulation remains a necessity for the existence of a privately-owned telecommunications company, the regulation Vail worked so hard to make effective – that is regulation by the individual states – is becoming increasingly inappropriate to the realities of a nation-wide and indeed international system. But the inevitable – and necessary – regulation by the Federal government has not been worked out by the Bell System and has instead been fought by it through the kind of delaying action Vail was so careful not to engage in.

As to Sloan's decentralization of General Motors it still stands – but it is becoming clear that it will have to be thought through again soon. Not only have basic principles of his design been changed and revised so often that they have become fuzzy beyond recognition: the autonomous automotive divisions, for instance, increasingly are not in full control of their manufacturing and assembly operations and therefore not fully responsible for the results. The individual makes of car, from Chevrolet to Cadillac, have also long ceased to represent major price classes the way Sloan originally designed them. Above all, Sloan designed a U.S. company – and though it soon acquired foreign subsidiaries, it remained a U.S. company in its organization and management structure. But General Motors is clearly an international company today. Its great growth and major opportunities are increasingly outside the United States and especially in Europe. It will survive and prosper only if it finds the right principles and the right organization for the multi-national company. The job Sloan did in 1922 will have to be done over again soon – it will predictably become pressing as soon as the industry runs into a period of economic difficulties. And if not done over fairly drastically, Sloan's solution is likely to become a millstone around GM's neck and increasingly a bar to its success.

When General Eisenhower was elected president, his predecessor, Harry S. Truman, said: 'Poor Ike; when he was a general, he gave an order and it was carried out. Now he is going to sit in that big office and he'll give an order and not a damn thing is going to happen.'

The reason why 'not a damn thing is going to happen' is, however, not that generals have more authority than presidents. It is that military organizations learned long ago that futility is the lot of most orders and organized the feedback to check on the execution of the order. They learned long ago that to go oneself and look is the only reliable feedback. Reports – all a president is normally able to mobilize – are not much help.* All military services have long ago learned that the officer who has given an order goes out and sees for himself whether it has been carried out.

* This was certainly established military practice in very ancient times – Thucydides and Xenophon both take it for granted, as do the earliest Chinese texts on war we have – and so did Caesar.

At the least he sends one of his own aides – he never relies on what he is told by the subordinate to whom the order was given. Not that he distrusts the subordinate; he has learned from experience to distrust communications.

This is the reason why a battalion commander is expected to go out and taste the food served his men. He could, of course, read the menus and order this or that item to be brought in to him. But no; he is expected to go into the mess hall and take his sample of the food from the same kettle that serves the enlisted men.

With the coming of the computer this will become even more important, for the decision-maker will, in all likelihood, be even further removed from the scene of action. Unless he accepts, as a matter of course, that he had better go out and look at the scene of action, he will be increasingly divorced from reality. All a computer can handle are abstractions. And abstractions can be relied on only if they are constantly checked against the concrete. Otherwise, they are certain to mislead.

To go and look for oneself is also the best, if not the only, way to test whether the assumptions on which a decision had been made are still valid or whether they are becoming obsolete and need to be thought through again. And one always has to expect the assumptions to become obsolete sooner or later. Reality never stands still very long.

Failure to go out and look is the typical reason for persisting in a course of action long after it has ceased to be appropriate or even rational. This is true for business decisions as well as for governmental policies. It explains in large measure the failure of Stalin's post-war policy in Europe but also the inability of the United States to adjust its policies to the realities of de Gaulle's Europe or the failure of the British to accept, until too late, the reality of the European Common Market.

One needs organized information for the feedback. One needs reports and figures. But unless one builds one's feedback around direct exposure to reality – unless one disciplines oneself to go out and look – one condemns oneself to a sterile dogmatism and with it to ineffectiveness.

These are the elements of the decision-process. But what about the decision itself?

7

Effective Decisions

A decision is a judgment. It is a choice between alternatives. It is rarely a choice between right and wrong. It is at best a choice between 'almost right' and 'probably wrong' – but much more often a choice between two courses of action neither of which is provably more nearly right, than the other.

Most books on decision-making tell the reader: 'First find the facts.' But executives who make effective decisions know that one does not start with facts. One starts with opinions. These are, of course, nothing but untested hypotheses and, as such, worthless, unless tested against reality. To determine what is a fact requires first a decision on the criteria of relevance, especially on the appropriate measurement. This is the hinge of the effective decision, and usually its most controversial aspect.

Finally, the effective decision does not, as so many texts on decision-making proclaim, flow from a consensus on the facts. The understanding that underlies the right decision grows out of the clash and conflict of divergent opinions and out of the serious consideration of competing alternatives.

To get the facts first is impossible. There are no facts unless one has a criterion of relevance. Events by themselves are not facts.

> In physics the taste of a substance is not a fact. Nor, until fairly recently, was its colour. In cooking, the taste is a fact of supreme importance, and in painting, the colour matters. Physics, cooking, and painting consider different things as relevant and therefore consider different things to be facts.

But the effective executive also knows that people do not start out with the search for facts. They start out with an opinion. There is nothing wrong with this. People experienced in an area should be expected to have an opinion. Not to have an opinion after having been exposed to an area for a good long time would argue an unobservant eye and a sluggish mind. People therefore inevitably start out with an opinion; to ask them to search for the facts first is even undesirable. They will simply do what everyone is far too prone to do anyhow: look for the facts that fit the conclusion they have already reached. And no one has ever failed to find the facts he is looking for. The good statistician knows this and distrusts all figures – he either knows the fellow who found them or he does not know him; in either case he is suspicious.

The only rigorous method, the only one that enables us to test an opinion against reality, is based on the clear recognition that opinions come first – and that this is the way it should be. Then no one can fail to see that we start out with untested hypotheses – in decision-making as in science the only starting point. We know what to do with hypotheses – one does not argue them; one tests them. One finds out which hypotheses are tenable, and therefore worthy of serious consideration, and which are eliminated by the first test against observable experience.

The effective executive encourages opinions. But he insists that the people who voice them also think through what it is that the 'experiment' – that is, the testing of the opinion against reality – would have to show. The effective executive, therefore, asks: 'What do we have to know to test the validity of this hypothesis? What would the facts have to be to make this opinion tenable?' And he makes it a habit – in himself and in the people with whom he works – to think through and spell out what needs to be looked at, studied, and tested. He insists that people who voice an opinion also take responsibility for defining what factual findings can be expected and should be looked for.

Perhaps the crucial question here is: 'What is the criterion of relevance?' This, more often than not, turns on the measurement appropriate to the matter under discussion and to the decision to be reached. Whenever one analyses the way a truly effective, a truly right decision has been reached, one finds that a great deal of work and thought went into finding the appropriate measurement.

> This, of course, is what made Theodore Vail's conclusion that service was the business of the Bell System such an effective decision.

The effective decision-maker assumes that the traditional measurement is not the right measurement. Otherwise, there would generally be no need for a decision; a simple adjustment would do. The traditional measurement reflects yesterday's decision. That there is need for a new one normally indicates that the measurement is no longer relevant.

That the procurement and inventory policies of the U.S. armed services were in bad shape had been known ever since the Korean War. There had been countless studies – but things got worse, rather than better. When Robert McNamara was appointed Secretary of Defence by President Kennedy, however, he challenged the traditional measurements of military inventory – measurements in total dollars and in total number of items in procurement and inventory. Instead, Mr McNamara identified and separated the very few items – maybe 4 per cent of the items by number – which together account for 90 per cent or more of the total procurement dollars. He similarly identified the very few items – perhaps again 4 per cent – which account for 90 per cent of combat readiness. Since some items belong in both categories, the list of crucial items came to 5 or 6 per cent of the total, whether measured by numbers or by dollars. Each of these, McNamara insisted, had to be managed separately and with attention to minute detail. The rest, the 95 per cent or so of all items which account neither for the bulk of the dollars nor for essential combat readiness, he changed to management by exception, i.e. to management by probability and averages. The new measurement immediately made possible highly effective decisions on procurement and inventory-keeping and on logistics.

The best way to find the appropriate measurement is again to go out and look for the 'feedback' discussed earlier – only this is 'feedback' before the decision.

In most personnel matters, for instance, events are measured in 'averages', such as the average number of lost-time accidents per hundred employees, the average percentage of absenteeism in the whole work force, or the average illness rate per hundred. But the executive who goes out and looks for himself will soon find that he needs a different measurement. The averages serve the purposes of the insurance company, but they are meaningless, indeed misleading, for personnel management decisions.

The great majority of all accidents occur in one or two places in the plant. The great bulk of absenteeism is in one department. Even illness resulting in absence from work, we now know, is not distributed as an average but is concentrated in a very small part of the work force, e.g. young unmarried women. The personnel actions to which dependence on the averages will lead, for instance the typical plant-wide safety campaign, will not produce the desired results, may indeed make things worse.

Similarly, failure to go and look was a major factor in the failure of the automobile industry to realize in time the need for safety-engineering of the car. The automobile companies measured only by the conventional averages of number of accidents per passenger mile or per car. Had they gone out and looked, they would have seen the need to measure also the severity of bodily injuries resulting from accidents. And this would soon have highlighted the need to supplement their safety campaigns by measures aimed at making the accident less dangerous, that is, by automotive design.

Finding the appropriate measurement is thus not a mathematical exercise. It is a risk-taking judgment.

Whenever one has to judge, one must have alternatives among which one can choose. A judgment in which one can only say 'yes' or 'no' is no judgment at all. Only if there are alternatives can one hope to get insight into what is truly at stake.

Effective executives therefore insist on alternatives of measurement – so that they can choose the one appropriate one.

There are a number of measurements for a proposal on a capital investment. One of these focuses on the length of time it will take before the original investment has been earned back. Another one focuses on the rate of profitability expected from the investment. A third one focuses on the present value of the returns expected to result from the investment, and so on. The effective executive will not be content with any one of these conventional yardsticks, no matter how fervently his accounting department assures him that only one of them is 'scientific'. He knows, if only from experience, that each of these analyses brings out a different aspect of the same capital investment decision. Until he has looked at each possible dimension of the decision, he cannot really know which of these ways of analysing and measuring is appropriate to the specific capital decision before him. Much as it annoys the accountants, the effective executive will insist on having the same investment decision calculated in all three ways – so as to be able to say at the end: '*this* measurement is appropriate to *this* decision.'

Unless one has considered alternatives, one has a closed mind.

This, above all, explains why effective decision-makers deliberately disregard the second major command of the text-books on decision-making and create dissension and disagreement, rather than consensus.

Decisions of the kind the executive has to make are not made well by acclamation. They are made well only if based on the clash of conflicting views, the dialogue between different points of view, the choice between different judgments. The first rule in decision-making is that one does not make a decision unless there is disagreement.

> Alfred P. Sloan is reported to have said at a meeting of one of his top committees: 'Gentlemen, I take it we are all in complete agreement on the decision here.' Everyone around the table nodded assent. 'Then,' continued Mr Sloan, 'I propose we postpone further discussion of this matter until our next meeting to give ourselves time to develop disagreement and perhaps gain some understanding of what the decision is all about.'

Sloan was anything but an 'intuitive' decision-maker. He always emphasized the need to test opinions against facts and the need to make absolutely sure that one did not start out with the conclusion and then look for the facts that would support it. But he knew that the right decision demands adequate disagreement.

Every one of the effective presidents in American history has had his own method of producing the disagreement he needed in order to make an effective decision. Lincoln, Theodore Roosevelt, Franklin D. Roosevelt, Harry Truman – each had his own ways – but each created the disagreement he needed for 'some understanding of what the decision is all about'. Washington, we know, hated conflicts and quarrels and wanted a united cabinet. Yet he made quite sure of the necessary differences of opinion on important matters by asking both Hamilton and Jefferson for their opinion.

> The President who understood best the need for organized disagreement was probably Franklin D. Roosevelt. Whenever anything of importance came up, he would take aside one of his aides and say to him, 'I want you to work on this for me – but keep it a secret.' (This made sure, as Roosevelt knew perfectly well, that everybody in Washington heard about it immediately.) Then Roosevelt would take aside a few other men, known to differ from the first and would give them the same assignment,

again 'in the strictest confidence'. As a result, he could be reasonably certain that all important aspects of every matter were being thought through and presented to him. He could be certain that he would not become the prisoner of somebody's preconceived conclusions.

This practice was severely criticized as execrable administration by the one 'professional manager' in Roosevelt's cabinet, his Secretary of the Interior, Harold Ickes, whose diaries are full of diatribes against the President's 'sloppiness', 'indiscretions', and 'treachery'. But Roosevelt knew that the main task of an American president is not administration. It is the making of policy, the making of the right decisions. And these are made best on the basis of 'adversary proceedings' to use the term of the lawyers for their method of getting at the true facts in a dispute, and of making sure that all relevant aspects of a case are presented to the Court.

There are three main reasons for the insistence on disagreement. It is, first, the only safeguard against the decision-maker's becoming the prisoner of the organization. Everybody always wants something from the decision-maker. Everybody is a special pleader, trying – often in perfectly good faith – to obtain the decision he favours. This is true whether the decision-maker is the President of the United States or the most junior engineer working on a design-modification.

The only way to break out of the prison of special pleading and pre-conceived notions is to make sure of argued, documented, thought-through disagreements.

Secondly, disagreement alone can provide alternatives to a decision. And a decision without an alternative is a desperate gambler's throw, no matter how carefully thought through it might be. There is always a high possibility that the decision will prove wrong – either because it was wrong to begin with or because a change in circumstances makes it wrong. If one has thought through alternatives during the decision-making process, one has something to fall back on, something that has already been thought through, that has been studied, that is understood. Without such an alternative, one is likely to flounder dismally when reality proves a decision to be inoperative.

In the last chapter I referred to both the Schlieffen Plan of the German Army in 1914 and President Franklin D. Roosevelt's original economic programme. Both were disproven by events at the very moment when they should have taken effect.

The German army never recovered. It never formulated another strategic concept. It went from one ill-conceived improvisation to the next. But this was inevitable. For twenty-five years no alternatives to the Schlieffen Plan had been considered by the General Staff. All its skills had gone into working out the details of this master plan. When the plan fell to pieces nobody had an alternative to fall back on. Despite all their careful training in strategic planning, the generals could only improvise, that is, dash off first in one direction and then in another without any real understanding why they dashed off in the first place.

Another 1914 event also shows the danger of having no alternative. After the Russians had ordered mobilization, the Tsar had second thoughts. He called in his Chief of Staff and asked him to halt the mobilization. 'Your Majesty,' the general answered, 'this is impossible; there is no plan for calling off the mobilization once it has started.' I do not believe that World War I would necessarily have been averted had the Russians been able to stop their military machine at the last moment. But there would have been one last chance for sanity.

By contrast, President Roosevelt, who in the months before he took office, had based his whole campaign on the slogan of economic orthodoxy, had a team of very able people, the later 'Brains Trust', working on an alternative, a radical policy, based on the proposals of the old-time 'Progressives', and aimed at economic and social reform on a grand scale. When the collapse of the banking system made it clear that economic orthodoxy had become political suicide, Roosevelt had his alternative ready. He therefore had a policy.

Yet without a prepared alternative, Roosevelt was as totally lost as the German General Staff or the Tsar of the Russians. When he assumed the presidency, Roosevelt was committed to conventional nineteenth-century theory for the international economy. Between his election in November 1932, however, and his taking office the following March, the bottom fell out of the international economy just as much as it had fallen out of the domestic economy. Roosevelt clearly saw this but, without alternatives, he was reduced to impotent improvisation. And even as able and agile a man as President Roosevelt could only grope around in what suddenly had become total fog, could only swing wildly from one extreme to another – as he did when he torpedoed the London Economic Conference; could only become the prisoner of the economic snake-oil salesmen with their patent nostrums such as dollar devaluation or the re-monetization of silver – both totally irrelevant to any of the real problems.

An even clearer example was Roosevelt's plan to 'pack' the Supreme Court after his landslide victory in 1936. When this plan ran into strong opposition in a Congress which he thought he controlled completely, Roosevelt had no alternative. As a result, he not only lost his plan for Court reform. He lost control of domestic politics – despite his towering popularity and his massive majorities.

Above all, disagreement is needed to stimulate the imagination. One does not, to be sure, need imagination to find the right answer to a problem. But then this is of value only in mathematics. In all matters of true uncertainty such as the executive deals with – whether his sphere is political, economic, social or military – one needs creative solutions which create a new situation. And this means that one needs imagination – a new and different way of perceiving and understanding.

Imagination of the first order is, I admit, not in abundant supply. But neither is it as scarce as is commonly believed. Imagination needs to be challenged and stimulated, however, or else it remains latent and unused. Disagreement, especially if forced to be reasoned, thought through, documented, is the most effective stimulus we know.

Few people have the White Queen's ability to believe a great many impossible things before breakfast. And still fewer have the imagination of the White Queen's creator, Lewis Carroll, the author of *Alice in Wonderland*. But even very small children have the imagination to enjoy Alice. And as Jerome S. Bruner* points out, even an eight-year-old sees in a flash that while '4 × 6 equals 6 × 4, a blind Venetian isn't the same thing as a Venetian blind'. This is imaginative insight of a high order. Far too many adult decisions are made on the assumption that a 'blind Venetian' must indeed be the same as a 'Venetian blind'.

* In his perceptive book, *Toward a Theory of Instruction* (Harvard, 1966).

An old story tells of a South Sea Islander of Victorian times who, after his return from a visit to the West, told his fellow-islanders that the Westerners had no water in their houses and buildings. On his native island water flowed through hollowed logs and was clearly visible. In the Western city it was conducted in pipes and, therefore, flowed only when someone turned a tap. But no one had explained the tap to the visitor.

Whenever I hear this story, I think of imagination. Unless we turn the 'tap', imagination will not flow. The tap is argued, disciplined disagreement.

The effective decision-maker, therefore, organizes disagreement. This protects him against being taken in by the plausible but false or incomplete. It gives him the alternatives so that he can choose and make a decision, but also so that he is not lost in the fog when his decision proves deficient or wrong in execution. And it forces the imagination – his own and that of his associates. Disagreement converts the plausible into the right and the right into the good decision.

The effective decision-maker does not start out with the assumption that one proposed course of action is right and that all others must be wrong. Nor does he start out with the assumption, 'I am right and he is wrong.' He starts out with the commitment to find out why people disagree.

Effective executives know, of course, that there are fools around and that there are mischief-makers. But they do not assume that the man who disagrees with what they themselves see as clear and obvious is, therefore, either a fool or a knave. They know that unless proven otherwise, the dissenter has to be assumed to be reasonably intelligent and reasonably fair-minded. Therefore, it has to be assumed that he has reached his so obviously wrong conclusion because he sees a different reality and is concerned with a different problem. The effective executive, therefore, always asks: 'What does this fellow have to see if his position were, after all, tenable, rational, intelligent?' The effective executive is concerned first with *understanding*. Only then does he even think about who is right and who is wrong.*

* This, of course, is nothing new. It is indeed only a re-phrasing of Mary Parker Follett (cf. her *Dynamic Administration*, edited by Metcalf and Urwick, London and New York, 1951), who in turn only extended Plato's arguments in his great dialogue on rhetoric, the *Phaedrus*.

In a good law office, the beginner, fresh out of law school, is first assigned to drafting the strongest possible case for the other lawyer's client. This is not only the intelligent thing to do before one sits down to work out the case for one's own client. (One has to assume after all, that the opposition's lawyer knows his business too.) It is also the right training for a young lawyer. It trains him not to start out with, 'I know why my case is right,' but with thinking through what it is that the other side must know, see, or take as probable to believe that it has a case at all. It tells him to see the two cases as alternatives. And only then is he likely to understand what his own case is all about. Only then can be made out a strong case in court that his alternative is to be preferred over the alternative the other side argues.

Needless to say, this is not done by a great many people, whether executives or not. Most people start out with the certainty that what they see is the only way to see at all.

The American steel executives have never raised the question: 'Why do these union people get so terribly exercised every time we mention the word "featherbedding?"' The union people in turn have never asked themselves why steel managements make such a fuss over featherbedding when every single instance thereof they have ever produced has proven to be petty, and irrelevant to boot. Instead, both sides have worked mightily to prove each other wrong. If either side had tried to understand what the other one sees and why, both would be a great deal stronger, and labour relations in the steel industry, if not in U.S. industry, would be a good deal better and healthier.

No matter how high his emotions run, no matter how certain he is that the other side is completely wrong and has no case at all, the executive who wants to make the right decision forces himself to see opposition as *his* means to think through the alternatives. He uses conflict of opinion as his tool to make sure all major aspects of an important matter are looked at carefully.

There is one final question the effective decision-maker asks: 'Is a decision really necessary?' *One* alternative is always the alternative of doing nothing.

Every decision is like surgery. It is an intervention into a system and therefore carries with it the risk of shock. One does not make unnecessary decisions any more than a good surgeon does unnecessary surgery. Individual decision-makers, like individual surgeons, differ in their styles. Some are more radical or more conservative than others. But by and large, they agree on the rules.

One has to make a decision when a condition is likely to degenerate if nothing is done. This also applies with respect to opportunity. If the opportunity is important and is likely to vanish unless one acts with dispatch, one acts – and one makes a radical change.

Theodore Vail's contemporaries agreed with him as to the degenerative danger of government ownership. But they wanted to fight it by fighting symptoms – fighting this or that bill in the legislature, opposing this or that candidate and supporting another, and so on. Vail alone understood that this is the ineffectual way to fight a degenerative condition. Even if one wins every battle, one can never win the war. He saw that drastic action was needed to create a new situation. He alone saw that private business had to make public regulation into an effective alternative to nationalization.

At the opposite end there are those conditions in respect to which one can, without being unduly optimistic, expect that they will take care of themselves even if nothing is done. If the answer to the question 'What will happen if we do nothing?' is 'It will take care of itself,' one does not interfere. Nor does one interfere if the condition, while annoying, is of no importance and unlikely to make any difference anyhow.

It is a rare executive who understands this. The controller who in a desperate financial crisis preaches cost reduction is seldom capable of leaving alone minor blemishes, elimination of which will achieve nothing. He may know, for instance, that the significant costs that are out of control are in the sales organization and in physical distribution. And he will work hard and brilliantly at getting them under control. But then he will discredit himself and the whole effort by making a big fuss about the 'unnecessary' employment of two or three old employees in an otherwise efficient and well-run plant. And he will dismiss as immoral the argument that eliminating these few semi-pensioners will not make any difference anyhow. 'Other people are making sacrifices,' he will argue, 'why should the plant people get away with inefficiency?'

When it is all over, the organization will forget fast that he saved the business. They will remember, though, his vendetta against the two or three poor devils in the plant – and rightly so. '*De minimis non curat praetor*' (the magistrate does not consider trifles) said the Roman law almost two thousand years ago – but many decision-makers still need to learn it.

The great majority of decisions will lie between these extremes. The problem is not going to take care of itself; but it is unlikely to turn into degenerative malignancy either. The opportunity is only for improvement rather than for real change and innovation; but it is still quite considerable. If we do not act, in other words, we will in all probability survive. But if we do act, we will be better off.

In this situation the effective decision-maker compares effort and risk of action to risk of inaction. There is no formula for the right decision here. But the guide lines are so clear that decision in the concrete case is rarely difficult. They are:

- act if on balance the benefits greatly outweigh cost and risk; and
- act or do not act; but do not 'hedge' or compromise.

The surgeon who only takes out half the tonsils or half the appendix risks as much infection or shock as if he did the whole job. And he has not cured the condition, has indeed made it worse. He either operates or he doesn't. Similarly, the effective decision-maker either acts or he doesn't act. He does not take half-action. This is the one thing that is always wrong, and the one sure way not to satisfy the minimum specifications, the minimum boundary conditions.

The decision is now ready to be made. The specifications have been thought through, the alternatives explored, the risks and gains weighed. Everything is known. Indeed it is always reasonably clear by now what course of action must be taken. At this point the decision does indeed almost 'make itself'.

And it is at this point that most decisions are lost. It becomes suddenly quite obvious that the decision is not going to be pleasant, is not going to be popular, is not going to be easy. It becomes clear that a decision requires courage as much as it requires judgment. There is no inherent reason why medicines should taste horribly – but effective ones usually do. Similarly there is no inherent reason why decisions should be distasteful – but most effective ones are.

One thing the effective executive will not do at this point. He will not give in to the cry, 'Let's make another study.' This is the coward's way – and all the coward ever achieves is to die a thousand deaths when the brave man dies one. When confronted with the demand for 'another study' the effective executive asks: 'Is there any reason to believe that additional study will produce anything new? And is there reason to believe that the new is likely to be relevant?' And if the answer is 'no' – as it usually is – the effective executive does not permit another study. He does not waste the time of good people to cover up his own indecision.

But at the same time, he will not rush into a decision unless he is sure he understands it. Like any reasonable experienced adult, he has learned to pay attention to what Socrates called his 'daemon': the inner voice, someplace in the bowels, that whispers: 'Take care.' Just because something is difficult, disagreeable, or frightening is no reason for not doing it, if it is right. But one holds back – if only for a moment – if one finds oneself uneasy, perturbed, bothered without quite knowing why. 'I always stop when things seem out of focus,' is the way one of the best decision-makers of my acquaintance puts it.

Nine times out of ten the uneasiness turns out to be some silly detail. But the tenth time one suddenly realizes that one has overlooked the most important fact in the problem, has made an elementary blunder, or has misjudged altogether. The tenth time one suddenly wakes up at night and realizes – as Sherlock Holmes did in the famous story – that the 'most significant thing is that the dog didn't bark'.

But the effective decision-maker does not wait long – a few days, at the most a few weeks. If the 'daemon' has not spoken by then, he acts with speed and energy whether he likes to or not.

Executives are not paid for doing things they like to do. They are being paid for getting the right things done – most of all in their specific task, the making of effective decisions.

II. Decision-making and the Computer

Does all this still apply today when we have the computer? The computer, we are being told, will replace the decision-maker, at least in middle-management. It will make, in a few years, all the operating decisions – and fairly soon thereafter it will take over the strategic decisions too.

Actually the computer will force executives to make as true decisions what are today mostly made as on-the-spot adaptations. It will convert a great many people who traditionally have reacted rather than acted into genuine executives and decision-makers.

The computer is a potent tool of the executive. Like hammer or pliers – but unlike wheel or saw – it cannot do anything man cannot do. But it can do one human job – addition and subtraction – infinitely faster than man can do it. And, being a tool, it does not get bored, does not get tired, does not charge overtime. Like all tools that do better something man can do, the computer multiplies man's capacity (the other tools, such as the wheel, the aeroplane or the TV set that do something man cannot do at all, add a new dimension to man, i.e. extend his nature). But like all tools the computer can only do one or two things. It has narrow limitations. And it is the limitations of the computer that will force us to do as genuine decision what now is largely done as *ad hoc* adaptation.

The strength of the computer lies in its being a logic machine. It does precisely what it is programmed to do. This makes it fast and precise. It also makes it a total moron; for logic is essentially stupid. It is doing the simple and obvious. The human being, by contrast, is not logical; he is perceptual. This means that he is slow and sloppy. But he is also bright and has insight. The human being can adapt; that is, he can infer from scanty information or from no information at all what the total picture might be like. He can remember a great many things nobody has programmed.

A simple and a common area where the typical traditional manager acts by way of on-the-spot adaptation is the commonplace inventory and shipping decision. The typical district sales manager knows, albeit most inaccurately, that customer A usually runs his plant on a very tight schedule and would be in real trouble if a promised delivery did not arrive on time. He knows also that customer B usually has adequate inventories of materials and supplies and can presumably manage to get by for a few days even if a delivery were late. He knows that customer C is already annoyed at his company and is only waiting for a pretext to shift his purchases to another supplier. He knows that he can get additional supplies of one item by asking for them as a special favour from this or that man in the plant back home, and so on. And on the basis of these experiences, the typical district sales manager adapts and adjusts as he goes along.

The computer knows none of these things. At least it does not know them unless it has been specifically told that these are the facts that determine company policy toward consumer A or in respect to product B. All it can do is react the way it has been instructed and programmed. It no more makes 'decisions' than the slide-rule or the cash register. All it can do is to compute.

The moment a company tries to put inventory control on the computer, it realizes that it has to develop rules. It has to develop an inventory *policy*. As soon as it tackles this, it finds that the basic decisions in respect to inventory are not inventory decisions at all They are highly risky business decisions. Inventory emerges as a means of balancing different risks: the risk of disappointing customer expectations in respect to delivery and service; the risk and cost of turbulence and instability in manufacturing schedules; and the risk and cost of locking up money in merchandise which might spoil, become obsolete, or otherwise deteriorate.

The traditional cliches do not greatly help. 'It is our aim to give 90 per cent of our customers 90 per cent fulfilment of delivery promises' sounds precise. It is actually meaningless, as one finds out when one tries to convert it into the step-by-step moron-logic of the computer. Does it mean that all our customers are expected to get 9 out of 10 orders when we promised them? Does it mean that our really good customers should get fulfilment all the time on all their orders – and how do we define a 'really good customer' anyhow? Does it mean that we aim to give fulfilment of these promises on all our products – or only on the major ones which together account for the bulk of our production? And what policy, if any, do we have with respect to the many hundreds of products which are not major for us, though they might well be major for the customer who orders one of them?

Each of these questions requires a risk-taking decision and, above all, a decision on principle. Until all these decisions have been made, the computer cannot control inventory. They are decisions of uncertainty – and what is relevant to them could not even be defined clearly enough to be conveyed to the computer.

To the extent, therefore, to which the computer – or any similar tool – is expected to keep operations on an even keel or to carry out predetermined reactions to expected events (whether the appearance of hostile nuclear missiles on the far horizon or the appearance of a crude oil with an unusual sulphur content in the petroleum refinery) the decision has to be anticipated and thought through. It can no longer be improvised. It can no longer be groped for in a series of small adaptations, each specific, each approximate, each, to use the physicist's terminology, a 'virtual' rather than a real decision. It has to be a decision in *principle*.

The computer is not the cause of this. The computer, being a tool, is probably not the cause of anything. It only brings out in sharp relief what has been happening all along. For this shift from the small adaptation to the decision in principle has been going on for a long time. It became particularly apparent during World War II and after, in the military. Precisely because military operations became so large and interdependent, requiring, for instance, logistics systems embracing whole theatres of operations and all branches of the armed services, middle-level commanders increasingly had to know the framework of strategic decisions within which they were operating. They increasingly had to make real decisions, rather than adapt their orders to local events. The second-level generals who emerged as the great men of World War II – a Rommel, a Bradley, a Zhukov – were all 'middle-managers' who thought through genuine decisions, rather than the dashing cavalry generals, the *beaux sabreurs* of earlier wars.

As a result, decision-making can no longer be confined to the very small group at the top. In one way or another almost every knowledge worker in an organization will either have to become a decision-maker himself or will at least have to be able to play an active, an intelligent and autonomous part in the decision-making process. What in the past had been a highly specialized function, discharged by a small and usually clearly defined organ – with the rest adapting within a mould of custom and usage – is rapidly becoming a normal if not an everyday task of every single unit in this new social institution, the large-scale knowledge organization. The ability to make effective decisions increasingly determines the ability of every knowledge worker, at least of those in responsible positions, to be effective altogether.

A good example of the shift to decision which the new techniques impose on us is the much discussed PERT (Programme

Evaluation and Review Technique) which aims at providing a 'road map' for the critical tasks in a highly complex programme such as the development and construction of a new space vehicle. PERT aims at giving control of such a programme by advance planning of each part of the work, of its sequence, and of the deadlines each part has to meet for the whole programme to be ready on time. This sharply curtails *ad hoc* adaptation. In its place there are high-risk decisions. The first few times operating men have to work out a PERT schedule, they are invariably wrong in almost every one of their judgments. They are still trying to do, through *ad hoc* adaptations, what can only be done through systematic risk-taking decision-making.

The computer has the same impact on strategic decisions. It cannot make them, of course. All it can do – and even that is potential rather than actual so far – is to work through what conclusions follow from certain assumptions made regarding an uncertain future, or conversely, what assumptions underlie certain proposed courses of action. Again, all it can do is compute. For this reason it demands clear analysis, especially of the boundary conditions the decision has to satisfy. And that requires risk-taking judgment of a high order.

There are additional implications of the computer for decision-making. If properly used, for instance, it should free senior executives from much of the pre-occupation with events inside the organization to which they are now being condemned by the absence or tardiness of reliable information. It should make it much easier for the executive to go and look for himself on the outside, that is, in the area where alone an organization can have results.

The computer might also change one of the typical mistakes in decision-making. Traditionally we have tended to err toward treating generic situations as a series of unique events. Traditionally we have tended to doctor symptoms. The computer, however, can only handle generic situations – this is all logic is ever concerned with. Hence we may well in the future tend to err by handling the exceptional, the unique, as if it were a symptom of the generic.

This tendency underlies the complaints that we are trying to substitute the computer for the proven and tested judgment of the military man. This should not be lightly dismissed as the grumbling of brass-hats. The most cogent attack on the attempt to standardize military decisions was made by an outstanding civilian 'management scientist', Sir Solly Zuckermann, the eminent biologist, who as scientific adviser to the British Ministry of Defence has played a leading part in the development of computer analysis and operational research.

The greatest impact of the computer lies in its limitations, which will force us increasingly to make decisions, and above all, force middle-managers to change from operators into executives and decision-makers.

This should have happened anyhow. One of the great strengths of such organizations as, for instance, General Motors among business firms, or the German General Staff among military groups, was precisely that these organizations long ago organized operating events as true decisions.

The sooner operating managers learn to make decisions as genuine judgments on risk and uncertainty, the sooner we will overcome one of the basic weaknesses of large organization – the absence of any training and testing for the decision-making top positions. As long as we can handle the events on the operating level by adaptation rather than by thinking, by 'feel' rather than by knowledge and analysis, operating people – in government, in the military or in business – will be untrained, untried, and untested when, as top executives, they are first confronted with strategic decisions.

The computer will, of course, no more make decision-makers out of clerks than the slide-rule makes a mathematician out of a high school student. But the computer will force us to make an early distinction between the clerk and the potential decision-maker. And it will permit the latter – may indeed force him – to learn purposeful, effective decision-making. For unless someone does this, and does it well, the computer cannot compute.

There is indeed ample reason why the appearance of the computer has sparked interest in decision-making. But the reason is not that the computer will 'take over' the decision. The reason is that with the computer taking over computation, people all the way down the line in the organization will have to learn to be executives and to make effective decisions.

Conclusion: Effectiveness Must be Learned

This book rests on two premises:

- the executive's job is to be effective; and
- effectiveness can be learned.

The executive is paid for being effective. He owes effectiveness to the organization for which he works. What then does the executive have to learn and have to do, to deserve being an executive? In trying to answer this question, this book has, on the whole, taken organizational performance and executive performance to be goals in and by themselves.

Effectiveness can be learned, is the second premise. The book has therefore tried to present the various dimensions of executive performance in such sequence as to stimulate readers to learn for themselves how to become effective executives. This is not a textbook, of course – if only because effectiveness, while capable of being learned, surely cannot be taught. Effectiveness is, after all, not a 'subject', but a self-discipline. But throughout this book and implicit in its structure and in the way it treats its subject matter is always the question: 'What makes for effectiveness in an organization and in any of the major areas of an executive's day and work?' Only rarely is the question asked: 'Why should there be effectiveness?' The goal of effectiveness is taken for granted.

In looking back on the arguments and flow of these chapters and on their findings, another and quite different aspect of executive effectiveness emerges, however. Effectiveness reveals itself as crucial to

- a man's self-development; to
- organization development; and to
- the fulfilment and viability of modern society.

1. The first step toward effectiveness is a procedure: *recording where the time goes*. This is mechanical if not mechanistic. The executive need not even do this himself – it is better done by a secretary or assistant. Yet if this is all the executive ever does, he will reap a substantial improvement. The results should be fast, if not immediate. If done with any continuity, recording one's time

will also prod and nudge a man toward the next steps for greater effectiveness.

Both the *analysis of the executive's time* and the elimination of the unnecessary time-wasters already requires some action. It requires some decisions. It requires some changes in a man's behaviour, his relationships, and his concerns. It raises searching questions regarding the relative importance of different uses of time, of different activities and of their goals. It should affect the level and the quality of a good deal of work done. Yet this can perhaps still be done by going down a checklist every few months, that is, by following a form. It still concerns itself only with efficiency in the utilization of a scarce resource, namely, time.

2. The next step, however, in which the executive is asked to focus his work on *outward contribution* advances from the procedural to the conceptual, from mechanics to analysis, and from efficiencies to concern with results. In this step the executive disciplines himself to think through the reason why he is on the payroll and the contribution he ought to make. There is nothing very complicated about this. The questions the executive asks himself about his contribution are still straightforward and more or less schematic. But the answers to these questions should lead to high demands on himself, to thinking about his own goals and those of the organization, and to concern with values. They should lead to demands on himself for high standards. Above all, these questions ask the executive to assume responsibility, rather than to act the subordinate, satisfied if he only 'pleases the boss'. In focusing his work on upward contribution the executive, in other words, has to think through purpose and ends rather than means alone.

3. *Making Strengths Productive* is fundamentally an attitude expressed in behaviour. It is fundamentally respect for the person – one's own as well as others. It is a value-system in action. But it is again 'learning through doing' and self-development through practice. In making strengths productive, the executive integrates individual purpose and organization needs, individual capacity and organization results, individual achievement and organization opportunity.

4. The chapter: *First Things First* serves as antiphon to the

earlier chapter, *Know Thy Time*. These two chapters might be called the twin pillars between which executive effectiveness is suspended and on which it rests. But the procedure here no longer deals with a resource, time, but with the end product, the performance of organization and executive. What is being recorded and analysed is no longer what happens to us but what we should try to make happen in the environment around us. And what is being developed here is not information, but character: foresight, self-reliance, courage. What is being developed here, in other words, is leadership – not the leadership of brilliance and genius, to be sure, but the much more modest yet more enduring leadership of dedication, determination, and serious purpose.

5. The *effective decision*, which the final chapters discuss, is concerned with rational action. There is no longer a broad and clearly marked path which the executive only has to walk down to gain effectiveness. But there are still clear surveyor's benchmarks to give orientation, and guidance how to get from one (of these benchmarks) to the next. How the executive, for instance, is to move from identifying a pattern of events as constituting a generic problem to the setting of the boundary conditions which the decision has to satisfy, is not spelled out. This has to be done according to the specific situation encountered. But what needs to be done and in what sequence should be clear enough. In following these benchmarks, the executive, it is expected, will develop and train himself in responsible judgment. Effective decision-making requires both procedure and analysis; but its essence is an ethics of action.

There is much more to the self-development of an executive than his training in effectiveness. He has to acquire knowledge and skills. He has to learn a good many new work habits as he proceeds along his career, and he will occasionally have to unlearn some old work habits. But knowledge, skills, and habits, no matter how accomplished, will avail the executive little unless he first develops himself in effectiveness.

There is nothing exalted about being an effective executive. It is simply doing one's job like thousands of others. There is little danger that anyone will compare this essay on training oneself in being an effective executive with, say, Kierkegaard's great self-development tract, *Training in Christianity*. There are surely higher goals for a man's life than to become an effective executive. But only because the goal is so modest can we hope at all to achieve it, that is, to have the large number of effective executives modern society and its organizations need. If we required saints, poets, or even first-rate scholars to staff our knowledge positions, the large-scale organization would simply be absurd and impossible. The needs of large-scale organization have to be satisfied by common people achieving uncommon performance. This is what the effective executive has to make himself able to do. Though this goal is a modest one, one that everyone should be able to reach if he works at it, the self-development of an effective executive is true development of the person. It goes from mechanics to attitudes, values, and character, from procedure to commitment.

Self-development of the effective executive is central to the development of the organization, whether it be a business, a government agency, a research laboratory, a hospital, or a military service. It is the way toward performance of the organization. As executives work toward becoming effective, they raise the performance level of the whole organization. They raise the sights of people – their own as well as others.

As a result, the organization not only becomes capable of doing better. It becomes capable of doing different things and of aspiring to different goals. Developing executive effectiveness will challenge directions, goals, and purposes of the organization. It raises the egos of its people from preoccupation with problems to a vision of opportunity, from concern with weakness to exploitation of strengths. This, in turn, wherever it happens, makes an organization attractive to people of high ability and aspiration and motivates people to higher performance and higher dedication. Organizations are not more effective because they have better people. They have better people because they motivate to self-development, through their standards, through their habits, through their climate. And these, in turn, result from systematic, focused, purposeful self-training of the individuals in becoming effective executives.

Modern society depends for its functioning, if not for its survival, on the effectiveness of large-scale organizations, on their performance and results, on their values, standards, and self-demands.

Organization performance has become decisive well beyond

the economic sphere or even the social sphere, for instance in education, in health-care, and in the advancement of knowledge. Increasingly the large-scale organization that counts is the knowledge-organization, employing knowledge workers and staffed heavily with men and women who have to perform as executives, men and women who have in their own work to assume responsibility for the results of the whole, and who, by the nature of their knowledge and work, make decisions with impact upon the results and performance of the whole.

Effective organizations are not common. They are even rarer than effective executives. There are shining examples here and there. But on the whole, organization performance is still primitive. Enormous resources are brought together in the modern large business, in the modern large government agency, in the modern large hospital or in the university; yet far too much of the result is mediocrity, far too much is splintering of efforts, far too much is devoted to yesterday or to avoiding decision and action. Organizations as well as executives need to work systematically on effectiveness and need to acquire the habit of effectiveness. They need to learn to feed their opportunities and to starve their problems. They need to work on making strength productive. They need to concentrate and to set priorities instead of trying to do a little bit of everything.

But executive effectiveness is surely one of the basic requirements of effective organization and in itself a most important contribution toward organization development.

Executive effectiveness is our one best hope to make modern society productive economically and viable socially.

The knowledge worker, as has been said again and again in this book, is rapidly becoming the major resource of the developed countries. He is becoming the major investment; for education is the most expensive investment of them all. He is becoming the major cost centre. To make the knowledge worker productive is the specific economic need of an industrially developed society. In such a society, the manual worker is not competitive in his costs with manual workers in underdeveloped or developing countries. Only productivity of the knowledge worker can make it possible for developed countries to maintain their high standard of living against the competition of low-wage developing economies.

So far, only a super-optimist would be reassured as to the productivity of the knowledge worker in the industrially developed countries. The tremendous shift of the centre of gravity in the work force from manual to knowledge work that has taken place since World War II has not, I submit, shown extraordinary results. By and large, neither the increase in productivity, nor the increase in profitability – the two yardsticks that measure economic results – have shown marked acceleration. No matter how well the industrially developed countries have done since World War II – and their record has been impressive – the job of making the knowledge worker productive is still ahead. The key to it is surely the effectiveness of the executive. For the executive is himself the decisive knowledge worker. His level, his standards, his demands on himself determine to a large extent the motivation, the direction, the dedication of the other knowledge workers around him.

Even more important is the social need for executive effectiveness. The cohesion and strength of our society depend increasingly on the integration of the psychological and social needs of the knowledge worker with the goals of organization and of industrial society.

The knowledge worker normally is not an economic problem. He tends to be affluent. He has high job security and his very knowledge gives him freedom to move. But his psychological needs and personal values need to be satisfied in and through his work and position in organization. He is considered – and considers himself – a professional. Yet he is an employee and under orders. He is beholden to a knowledge area, yet he has to subordinate the authority of knowledge to organizational objectives and goals. In a knowledge area there are no superiors or subordinates, there are only older and younger men. Yet organization requires a hierarchy. These are not entirely new problems, to be sure. Officer Corps and Civil Service have known them for a long time, and have known how to resolve them. But they are real problems. The knowledge worker is not poverty-prone. He is in danger of alienation to use the fashionable word for boredom, frustration, and silent despair.

Just as the economic conflict between the needs of the manual worker and the demands of an expanding economy was *the* social question of the nineteenth century in the developing countries, so the position, function, and fulfilment of the knowledge worker is the social question of the twentieth century in these countries now that they are developed.

It is not a question that will go away if we deny its existence. To assert (as do in their own way both orthodox economists and Marxists) that only the 'objective reality' of economic and social performance exists, will not make the problem go away. Nor, however, will the new romanticism of the social psychologists (e.g. Professor Chris Argyris at Yale) who quite rightly point out that organizational goals are not automatically individual fulfilment and therefrom conclude that we had better sweep them aside. We will have to satisfy *both* the objective needs of society for organization performance by the organization and the needs of the person for achievement and fulfilment.

Self-development of the executive towards effectiveness is the only integrator available. It is the only way in which organization goals and individual needs can come together. The executive who works at making strengths productive – his own as well as those of others – works at making organizational performance compatible with personal achievement. He works at making his knowledge area become organizational opportunity. And by focusing on upward contribution, he makes his own values become organization results.

The manual worker, so at least the nineteenth century believed, had only economic goals and was content with economic rewards. That, as the 'human relations' school demonstrated, was far from the whole truth. It certainly ceased to be true the moment pay went above the subsistence level. The knowledge worker demands economic rewards too. Their absence is a deterrent. But their presence is not enough. He needs opportunity, he needs achievement, he needs fulfilment, he needs values. Only by making himself an effective executive can the knowledge worker obtain these satisfactions. Only executive effectiveness can enable this society of ours to harmonize its two needs, the needs of organization to obtain from the individual the contribution it needs and the need of the individual to have organization serve as his tool for the accomplishment of his purposes.

Effectiveness *must* be learned.

Index

F/RUP001/320/4/05